MERRY CHRISTMAS.

GOD BLESS!

dys-
functional

the Rick Langlais story

ANDREW FEHR with Rick Langlais

Cover and book design by Fred Koop, Saskatoon, SK

Printed in Canada by Houghton Boston Printers, Saskatoon, SK

Library and Archives Canada Cataloguing in Publication

Fehr, Andrew, 1963-
    Dysfunctional : the Rick Langlais story / Andrew Fehr with Rick Langlais.

ISBN 978-0-9868096-0-6

    1. Langlais, Rick, 1959-. 2. Hands On Street Ministries. 3. Adult child abuse victims--Canada--Biography. 4. Adult child sexual abuse victims-- Canada--Biography. 5. Recovering addicts--Canada--Biography. 6. Lay ministry--Saskatchewan--Saskatoon--Biography. 7. Rescue missions (Church work)--Saskatchewan--Saskatoon. 8. City missions--Saskatchewan-- Saskatoon. I. Langlais, Rick, 1959- II. Title.

BV2657.L35F44 2010   266.022092   C2010-907969-8

"Therefore, God exalted him to the highest place and gave him the name that is above every other name, that at the name of Jesus every knee should bow, in heaven and on earth and under the earth, and every tongue confess that Jesus Christ is Lord, to the glory of God the Father."

PHILLIPIANS 2:9-11

Author's Preface

Over a period of several months in 2009 and 2010 I had the privilege of sitting down over coffee every Wednesday morning in my office with Rick Langlais. As he talked about his life I listened, took notes and prodded him with the occasional question. We cried, laughed and prayed together. He told me a number of times that the whole experience of sharing his life story was like peeling off layers of pain, heartache and regret that had hardened and scaled over the years. It now felt like the layers were being chiselled away piece by piece.

Some pieces came off easier than others, but slowly, as they fell away, an incredible story began to emerge. The story is incredible not only because Rick is an amazing fighter and survivor, although he certainly is – but because the God Rick came to know is an amazing God. This is a story that would have never been told, more than that, a life that would never have been lived, if not for the protecting and intervening hand of God. Through early years of unimaginable abuse, learning to survive on the streets, rising to the top as a drug dealer and enforcer, and abusing his own body with drugs and alcohol for decades, there was an invisible yet powerful hand watching over him.

This is not a pleasant or a polite story. It is a story of physical and sexual abuse, horrific violence and the raw ugliness of addiction. But it is also a story of incredible love and hope. From the bottom of his heart Rick believes that every human being, no matter how deeply entrenched they may be in cycles of abuse, addiction or corruption, is a person of immeasurable value. He believes that no one is ever beyond hope or beyond the reach of God's love.

For obvious reasons some names and places have been altered, and there are some parts of the story that simply cannot be told. But the events that are recorded are real.

Some of the events recorded in these pages will seem almost unbelievable, and I must admit that there were times when I found myself questioning Rick's recollection. However, I discovered as I travelled to several places Rick identified and interviewed a number of people who are part of his story, Rick has not overdramatized these events. If anything, the opposite is true. In order to show respect and to protect the dignity of certain individuals he has downplayed what really happened in many cases.

When I asked those who had witnessed Rick as a fighter to describe him, immediately it became obvious that they were, and still are, in awe of his abilities. Words like, "unbelievable," "amazing," "like nothing you can imagine," "fast" and "vicious," were used repeatedly. Rick's closest friends said that watching him was like watching someone in a martial arts movie, except that it was real, and Rick was better, faster and meaner than anyone you ever saw in a movie. Although his friends trusted him completely and never once had reason to question his loyalty, even those closest to him were at times afraid to be within arm's reach. He was volatile and dangerous.

In 1988 Rick's life took a radical turn when he met a pastor who introduced him to Jesus. The change since then, although not instant or at times even obvious, has been dramatic. Transformation is sometimes a long and painful road. For Rick that road has been filled with struggles, disappointments and ongoing battles with the addictions and inner demons he has fought since childhood.

In 1992 Rick opened Hands On Street Ministries in Saskatoon. Since that time his methods and mannerisms have sometimes been questioned. He is not a typical street minister and Hands On is not a typical street ministry. Occasionally this leads to misunderstandings and opens Rick up to harsh criticism, but his approach to ministry also opens up many doors, and gives him opportunities to reach out to those who would otherwise have nowhere else to turn. Rick is a unique individual who has chosen to use the gifts God has given him to minister in the best way he knows how, to the neediest and most vulnerable people in the inner city.

Whether or not you agree with his methods, you cannot question his motives or his heart. He understands the needs and the struggles of the people he ministers to perhaps better than anyone else. He knows because he's been there.

Rick often tells people that God is bigger than the boogeyman. Whatever boogeyman you are facing, there is a God who offers help, hope and grace without measure. Of that Rick is convinced. He is living proof.

CHAPTER 1

The earliest memory I have from my childhood is of my nose being broken.

Nearly five decades have passed, so the details are a bit sketchy, but I remember looking out the back window of a car and waving goodbye to my dad. Mom had piled all of us kids into the back seat, and she was taking us away to live with her new boyfriend, Al. I made a bit of a fuss because I didn't want to go, and the next thing I knew, the back of my mother's hand swung around and smashed into my face. The pain was excruciating. It felt like my nose had exploded.

"Sit down and shut up!" she yelled. Her voice and her eyes were filled with rage.

Someone handed me a rag to soak up the blood that was running down my face, and I sat there quietly holding my bleeding nose. I knew if I made even a whimper I would get hit again.

I was born on June 5, 1959 in Kenora, Ontario, the sixth of eight children. Carol was the oldest of the kids, but she didn't live with us, so I didn't even know about her until quite a few years later. After her came Maureen, Guy, Ray, Rena, me and then Larry and Roxanne. There were a couple of other boys named Lance and Dean who came and lived with us for a while too, but I was never sure whether or not they were my brothers. They're both dead now, so I guess I'll never know. Mom and Dad were both in and out of a number of relationships over the years, so to say we were a messed-up family is an understatement.

My parents named me Richard, but they called me Rocky, after the boxer, Rocky Marciano. Dad said it was because I came out fighting. The association with a fighter was more fitting than anyone could have known at the time.

I was a small, scrawny kid with dark hair and brown eyes. None of us kids were very big, but our mom, Doris, was a large woman. She was probably close to 200 lbs., and she was mean. Nobody messed with Doris. Our dad, Ray, was just a short man, but he was as tough as they came, built like a brick. Like him, I was always a bit on the small side. I probably heard people say a thousand times in my life, "I thought you'd be bigger." I got that a lot later on in life when people started to hear about me.

The day my nose was broken we moved a few hours away to the small village of Upsala, Ont. At that time the entire village consisted of a hotel, a corner store, and a small church. We lived a few miles out in the country in a big house with no plumbing or electricity. Mom and Al drank a lot, and it seemed to me that Mom was always mad about something. Violence and beatings were a part of my daily life.

I learned from a very early age that my mother hated me. She told me hundreds of times that she wished I was dead, or that I had never been born. She was filled with an uncontrollable rage. I don't know what I ever did to deserve it, but the brunt of her anger was usually directed at me. The other kids got slapped around too, but when she flew into one of her ugly furies I was the one she came looking for.

The only explanation she ever gave for the way she treated me was something she said years later when one of my sisters questioned her about it. She never indicated that she was sorry for what she did—she just made an excuse. "I was sick back then," she said. "I was sick, and he could take it. He never cried."

I'm not sure why I never cried when she beat me, but I think it was because that was the one part of me she couldn't control. She could beat me and throw me around and even knock me unconscious—there was nothing I could do about that. But I didn't have to let her break my spirit. I didn't have to let her see how much she was hurting me.

I guess she was threatened by that. If I was strong, it meant she was weak. So she beat me with her fists, and with her words. Physically and emotionally she hammered me down every day.

My memories from those early days in Upsala are mostly of being hit and kicked around, or of trying to keep quiet and stay out of sight. I learned it was best not to draw attention to myself. I don't ever remember being touched or held in a loving way. Not once was I ever hugged by anyone or told that I was loved.

One of my few early memories not involving a beating is when I ran into a black bear behind our house. On the back corner of our property was a scrap heap, where we threw all our garbage. As Al was doing some work on his car one afternoon he told me to get rid of a bucket of old oil, I walked up onto the trash pile and was about to give the pail a heave when I looked up and saw a bear just a few feet away. It was only a cub, but to a scrawny, five-year-old kid it looked absolutely huge! I ran back to Al in a panic and managed to stammer out, "B-b-b-bear." He got his gun, but when he saw how small the bear was, he didn't bother shooting it. He just laughed, and chased it away.

I could hardly wait for my brothers and sisters to get home from school that afternoon. By the time they came I had made up a big story about how I had yelled and ran at the giant bear and scared it off. I wanted them to know that not even a big old bear was any match for Rocky.

After living in Upsala for six months, we moved to Prince George, B.C., where we lived in a small, cheap, two-room motel suite for the next year. The living conditions there were awful. The seven of us kids slept in one room, and Mom and

Al in the other. Again, there wasn't any plumbing, so we had to use a bucket for a toilet.

It was there in Prince George that I got into my first real fight. Some boys from next door were picking on my older brother, Ray. The rest of us came to his rescue, and it turned into an all-out brawl. I was the smallest and youngest kid there, but I wasn't about to let little details like that stop me from getting into the middle of the action. During the fight, someone picked up a three-foot long chunk of board and swung it at my head. The board looked like it was part of an old wooden fence at one time, and it had a nail sticking out of one end. The nail sunk into the top of my head and got stuck there. I finished the fight and then walked home with the board still swinging from my head, and blood running down my face. I thought it was pretty cool.

Mom yanked out the nail and then brought me next door to show the neighbour lady what her boys had done to me. Some angry words were exchanged, and then we went back home. I understood clearly that day that the privilege of beating me was hers alone.

Ray was always getting us into trouble. If there was a commotion going on somewhere, no doubt Ray was in the middle of it. His amazingly creative imagination, together with the rage that was inside all of us, was a volatile combination that got us into some interesting situations. While we were living in Prince George, he went out one evening and started up a D9 CAT bulldozer that was parked at a construction site on the edge of town. After putting it in gear, he jumped off and ran back home. Later that night, we listened from our room as the irate contractor told Al and Mom about the thousands of dollars in damages that had been done by the runaway CAT. As we listened, tears streamed down our faces, because we were laughing so hard at what Ray had done and because we knew we were in for the beating of our lives. I looked at Ray, crying and laughing at the same time, and said, "We're really going to get it this time." We did. We got whipped that night with a skipping rope until our backs were bleeding and raw.

The following summer we packed up and moved back to Upsala, this time to a small house right behind the hotel. That seemed quite convenient to me, because Mom and Al spent most of their free time at the hotel bar anyway.

We moved back and forth several times in the coming years between B.C. and Ontario. I didn't mind the long drives, in fact, I actually liked them because, at least for that time, I wasn't being beaten. I was happy just to sit in the back seat and be left alone.

Back in Upsala I became friends with the hotel owner's son. He was a small, quiet kid like me, and we hit it off right away. He knew how to reach his arm inside the vending machine and trip the switch to get cigarettes. So, at age seven I started smoking. We would grab 10 or 12 packs of cigarettes and then run to the bush just outside of town, where we had built our secret fort. Our fort was just a little clearing underneath some brush, but it was our own private place where no one would bother us. There we would chain-smoke until we were so dizzy we would throw up. Then we'd smoke some more.

After a few months of living behind the hotel we moved again, this time to a farmhouse in the country. Al started to work in the bush, and his work sometimes took him away for several weeks at a time. The increased pressure of looking after seven kids by herself was too much for Mom—the beatings became even more frequent, and seemed to reach a new level of intensity.

Although we had an inside bathroom, we weren't allowed to use it very often. Instead, sometimes before she beat me Mom would order me to go to the outhouse, empty my bowels (she said it a bit cruder than that), and then when I was done, strip naked, and wait for her against the side of the house. That way I wouldn't get blood on my clothes or crap in my pants when I lost control of my faculties. She would sometimes grab a skipping rope and whip me, or she would just kick, slap, and punch me until I passed out. Other times, she would pick up whatever was handy and start hitting me with it, or grab me by the scruff of my neck and the back of my shirt and throw me around. It was kind of like the old TV bar room brawl scenes, except I was just a little kid and couldn't do anything to fight back or defend myself.

Sometimes she would drag me to the bathroom and beat my head against the toilet until I stopped fighting. Then she would press my face down into the bowl until I was unconscious. After a while, I learned that it was best if I didn't fight back too hard or too long. I learned to just protect the really sensitive parts of my face and body, and let her do what she was going to do. Whenever she was beating me, she always told me she hated me and wished I was dead.

When she really wanted to degrade me she would call me a dog. Sometimes when I was being treated like a dog, I wasn't allowed to eat at the table with the rest of the family. After the meal, the table scraps would be scraped on to a plate and she would force me to eat all of it. I hated the fat that was trimmed off the meat, but she would make me keep eating it until I threw up. I was like the family dog, except that our dog Bullet got treated better than I did—he took a lot less beatings than me, and at least he had a name. I didn't even have that. To my mother I was just "the dog."

When I was in third grade I hurt my arm one day while playing at school with some kids. There wasn't a hospital nearby, but the local store was run by a nurse. The pain in my arm was pretty bad, so Mom took me to see her after a couple of days. The nurse examined me and said it was most likely just a pinched nerve and would probably get better on its own over time. She gave Mom a tensor bandage and told her to wrap up my arm for the next while.

About a week later, that same arm was broken during a beating. I knew I was hurt seriously, but I didn't dare complain. In the coming days it started to swell up quite noticeably. Mom responded by just wrapping the tensor bandage even tighter to try to keep the swelling down. Every day my arm seemed to get a bit more swollen, with the pain becoming almost unbearable. After another week or so, it was bigger around than my leg, and was starting to fester inside the bandage. It eventually got to the point where I couldn't even get my arm inside Al's big lumber jacket. That's when Mom decided I could stay home from school.

Over the next couple of weeks it kept getting worse. My whole arm turned green and black, and it started to smell awful. One night, when my sister Maureen took the bandage off to have a look at it, some thick green slime started to ooze out. It was the vilest, most nauseating thing I had ever smelled. I was in bad shape, and I could feel myself starting to slip in and out of delirium.

The next morning, Maureen took the brunt of Mom's rage when she found out she had tried to help me. When my sister Rena went to school that day, she told the teacher I was hurt really bad and needed help. A couple of hours later, two policemen showed up at our house. When they saw the condition I was in, they put me in the back of their police cruiser right away and raced the two hours from Upsala to the nearest hospital, located in the town of Thunder Bay (but back then it was still called Port Arthur).

I was in a lot of pain. The whole way there the officer who sat in the back seat with me held me and told me I was going to be okay. I wanted so badly to believe him—I needed to believe him.

He stayed with me while I went for x-rays, and I remember thinking he was the nicest person I had ever met. After the x-rays, I heard the doctor telling him it didn't look good, and they would probably have to take my arm. When I heard those words I snapped. There was no way they were going to cut off my arm! I started to scream and (thrash) around on the table, and the policeman had to literally lie on top of me to restrain me. While I was lying there I could feel his heart beating as he put his arms around me and held me tight against his chest. I had never been held like that before, and I remember thinking it was strange to feel someone else's heartbeat. I was crying and screaming, and the policeman was crying, too. He begged the doctor to try to save my arm. "Give the kid a chance," he said.

"The kid's going to die if we don't take that arm," the doctor told him.

The policeman kept asking him to try, and finally I heard the doctor say he would see what he could do.

Today, the scar extending from the top of my arm to down below my elbow is a reminder of how bad the infection had become, and how close I came to losing that arm, or maybe even my life.

After I had stayed in the hospital for a couple of weeks, Al and Doris came to pick me up. Doris was my mom, but from that day on I started calling her Doris. It would be several years yet before I started calling her Doris to her face, because I knew that if she heard me say it, another beating would follow. But from then on, inside my head and whenever I talked about her to anyone else, she was Doris; she wasn't my mother anymore. I knew without a doubt that she literally hated me.

On the way home from the hospital we stopped at a restaurant, which was a brand-new experience for me—I had never been to a restaurant before. Al told me I could order whatever I wanted, so I ordered a plate of French fries, and smothered them with ketchup. I guess in their own way they were trying to make it up to me. Their intentions, at least for that moment, might have been good, but at home nothing changed. They were stuck in a hopeless cycle of violence, fueled by alcohol and drug abuse.

The doctor told me that although he had saved my arm, I would never be able to use it properly again. He might have been right, except for what my brother Guy did for me. After I came home, Guy worked with me every day to help me get movement and strength back into my arm. He put a handful of pennies into a sock and told me that if I kept lifting it every day, I could keep them. We didn't have much money—even pennies were hard to come by—so Guy would go out after school and search the ditches for beer bottles and pop bottles to cash in at the store. The coins he collected were added to the sock, and slowly it became heavier. Over the next few months I kept lifting that sock full of pennies, over and over again. Slowly I felt the strength beginning to return to my arm.

We didn't know what normal family life was like. Losing a fight at school was seen as a sign of weakness, and weakness wasn't tolerated at our house. The school we attended had two classrooms, one for the younger grades and the other one for the older kids. One of the bigger, older kids started picking on Guy, pushing him around and calling him names. This went on for a few weeks until one day he told Guy he was going to beat him up after school. We may not have had a normal family life at home, but we kids stuck together and stuck up for each other. So later that day during recess, Rena came up behind this kid while he was taking a drink from a water fountain and smashed his face down as hard as she could with her metal lunch kit. She did some pretty serious damage to his nose and lips, and knocked out one of his teeth. For us that was normal behaviour. That's how we handled our problems.

We boys were all bed-wetters. Of course, wetting the bed was always cause for a beating, so we came up with an alarm system for waking up to go to the bathroom. We took a piece of rope and tied one end to Ray's foot and the other end to a stack of books. Then we set the books on the shelf above him so that when he moved or rolled over in the middle of the night the books would crash down on him. Then he would wake up the rest of us, and we would all take turns going down the hall to the bathroom. (Ray was selected by process of elimination.) It was Guy's idea, so he said that since he was the brains behind the operation he had already done his part.) Larry was the smallest kid, I still had my arm in a cast, and it didn't seem right to make one of the girls do it. So Ray was chosen, but it didn't seem to matter to him; (he was always game for anything.) That was Ray.

Naturally, we got the biggest books we could find—some sort of encyclopedias—so he would be sure to wake up when they fell on him. The books were positioned to land on his legs, but sometimes they hit a little bit higher than the intended target area. We always knew when that happened, because Ray's language would be even more colourful than usual. I can still hear the dull "thud" of the books landing on Ray, followed by some swearing, and then the sound of my brothers and sisters getting up to go to the bathroom.

Sometimes the plan worked, but when it didn't work, Doris wrapped the wet sheets around my face and then hit and punched me. Then she made me scrub the sheets until they were clean. My nose was broken this way at least a couple of times. By my count, my nose was broken 12 times by the time I was 12 years old. On my 13th birthday it was broken again, when Doris shoved me down and then kicked me in the face while I was leaning against the fridge.

When your nose gets broken, it feels like your whole head is exploding. You first hear bones breaking, and then there's blood everywhere. You put your hands to your face and immediately they are filled with blood. Instantly your head is throbbing, your vision goes blurry and your eyes start to water and swell shut. Within a couple of minutes you're just looking through little slits in your eyelids. The blood doesn't just run out of your nose—it also runs down your throat, so you have to be careful not to swallow too much of it. If you do, you'll gag and then throw up. The throbbing, head-splitting pain is almost unbearable.

One day, while we were living in the farmhouse in the country, Ray and I found a huge gingerbread house in the attic. It was an amazing work of art, elaborately decorated with white icing and more candy than we had ever seen in one place. The roof was covered with Smarties, there was a candy cane fence, and the windows and walkway were lined with red, green, and yellow gumdrops. We weren't allowed to be in the attic because that's where the landlady stored some of her belongings, but telling us the attic was off-limits was all the more reason Ray needed to go up there.

Over the next several months, Ray and I reduced that gingerbread house to a few scattered crumbs. When Doris would get mad and send us from the table without any dinner, we would just smile at each other and head for the attic.

That Christmas when the landlady came for her gingerbread house, she wasn't impressed with what she found. Doris came right after us. When the landlady saw what was happening, she tried to downplay the situation. "It was just a gingerbread house," she said. "It's no big deal."

Big deal or not, after she left, our backs were once again whipped raw with a skipping rope. I remember the pain very well.

Late one night while I was lying awake in bed, I heard Al and Doris talking about me. Though she was yelling I still couldn't quite make out what she was saying, so I snuck over to the top of the stairs to hear a little better. She told Al she hated me and wished I was dead. That was nothing new, but she went on to say she didn't want me around anymore, and that if my dad wouldn't take me back, she was afraid she might kill me.

That scared me. Would she really kill me? From then on, I tried my best to become invisible. I stopped speaking, and did whatever I could to stay out of sight, but it didn't work. The beatings became even more vicious, and more and more often I would be beaten for seemingly nothing at all. It seemed like I was continually covered with bruises from head to toe.

A little while later, Ray was sent to live with our dad. Ray was becoming more violent and out of control, and was starting to get into trouble with the police. Doris said she just couldn't handle him anymore. With Ray gone, all of Doris' rage was focused directly on me. Until he left he had absorbed at least some of her attention, but with him out of the picture it was now all aimed in my direction. Again, I did my best to stay as invisible as possible, but not many days went by that I wasn't beaten.

A year after Ray left, Doris decided she had enough of the rest of us too, so she started making plans to send all of us to live with our dad. When I found out we were being sent away, I wrote her a letter, begging her to let me stay. In the letter I told her I was sorry for being bad, and I promised to try to be better.

Even with all the abuse, I didn't want to go. Early on, whenever we moved, I had hoped that with a fresh start maybe things would get better. But with each move the abuse had become even worse. So, once again I assumed I would be moving into a situation even worse than the one I was already in.

I couldn't bring myself to give her the letter because I thought it would lead to another beating, so I hid it in a storage trunk out on the porch. It turned out my hiding place wasn't chosen very well. The night before we were to leave, she came across it while packing up a few things to send with us.

That night as she sat on the edge of my bed, she explained, in the best way she could, that she just couldn't handle us anymore. For my own good she was sending me away because she was afraid of what might happen if I stayed. That was the one and only time I ever sensed any sort of decency in her.

The next morning we were put on a plane and shipped off to live with our dad in the town of Scotland, Ont. When we arrived at the airport, there were two men there to greet us. I was nine years old, and I hadn't seen my dad for nearly five years, so I wasn't sure which one was him. I took a guess, and went to stand next to one of them. When I realized I had guessed wrong I was afraid, so I went and stood beside the dog crate, and didn't say a word. I was hoping no one would notice me, because if no one noticed me, no one would hit me.

After a couple hours' drive we arrived at our new home and met our new "mom." Carol was a lot younger than our dad, but she'd been with him for a couple of years already. She had medium-length, brown hair and dark eyes. She was a very pretty young woman.

When we walked into the house the first thing we saw was the table piled high with food set out for us—sandwiches, meat, cheese and fruit. But even with all of that, I couldn't stop

Larry, Ray and Rena (in front, left to right), with me in the back, at Dad and Carol's house in Scotland, Ontario.

staring at the big freezer off to the side of the room. The top of the freezer was completely covered with homemade pies! I couldn't believe it! I had never seen anything like it before.

It was already late at night, but they told us we could eat whatever we wanted. I asked for a piece of pie, and Carol handed me a big slice of the most delicious blueberry pie I had ever tasted. It was amazing!

That night I really believed my life was going to get better. I dared to hope that the nightmare I had been living was over. From now on, life was going to be good. No more beatings, no more pain—I was going to be okay.

I was so very, very wrong. I remember that pie being unbelievably good though, and for that night, I was in heaven. I didn't know that more hell was coming.

CHAPTER 2

We must have been quite a sight, standing there in the airport—five skinny kids with a couple of bags of worn-out clothes and an old, half-blind dog. It wasn't what Dad and Carol were expecting, and it was more than they knew how to deal with. The day after we arrived, our dog Bullet got into a fight with their dog. It was a ferocious, bloody fight. We didn't know it at the time, but it was a picture of the chaos and violence that was ahead for all of us.

Dad and Carol tried—I'll give them credit for that. They too were caught up in a hopeless cycle of drugs, alcohol, and sexual and physical abuse, but I really believe that their intentions were good, at least for the first few days. As best as they knew how, and in spite of their addictions, they did try to make a home for us. They went out and bought us all new clothes, school supplies and toys, and they even took out a loan for a brand-new Chevy Impala. But it was clear from the start that they were in way over their heads.

For the past year it had just been the two of them and my brother Ray, and although Ray Jr. was constantly getting into some sort of trouble, they had at least been able to keep a small sense of order in the house. But with the added stress of five more kids to look after, and the extra financial pressure and debt they had just taken on, things turned ugly in a hurry.

Dad was working for a farmer who owned a 75-acre produce farm, and we were living in the old farmhouse. It was a huge house with a big kitchen and living room and a massive stairwell that led up to a balcony and six bedrooms. On the farm we grew potatoes, corn, squash, carrots, and a whole assortment of other vegetables and fruits. We arrived in early summer just when the strawberries were ripening, so we kids were sent out to the fields to pick them. I think we ended up putting just as many in our mouths as in the baskets. They were so good that we just couldn't stop eating. Did we ever get sick!

Dad soon realized that the upside of having more kids around was that suddenly there was plenty of free labour to be exploited. He put us to work hoeing, weeding and picking whatever vegetables were ready for the market.

A few months after we arrived, Dad started raising pigs. This brought in a bit more income, and also added to our work load. We would go through the fields that had been harvested and pick up whatever was left behind to feed to the pigs.

When the sows gave birth to their piglets there were sometimes runts that needed to be put down. Within a day or two you could always tell which ones were the runts because the rest of the litter would grow quickly, and they'd be left behind. Either there was something wrong with them or they were just smaller and weaker to begin with, so they got bullied and shoved off to the side and couldn't get the milk they needed from their mothers. Since they were going to die anyway, Dad would just get rid of them.

I felt sorry for the little runts. It didn't seem fair for them to be treated that way. So, one day I rescued one of them and brought him up to the hayloft in the top of the barn. I built a little fort with straw bales and kept him hidden there. He was cute and soft, and liked to cuddle up against my face when I talked to him. I named him Scottie, because he reminded me of "Scottie's Little Softie" from the TV commercials. When no one was around, I'd take him down to his mother so he got some milk to drink, and then quickly hide him away again in the loft. There were a couple of times when I almost got caught, but I managed to sneak him away before Dad found him. I spent hours up there talking to Scottie and cuddling with him. I loved him just as much as any kid has ever loved a pet.

After a few weeks he was getting too big and loud to keep up there anymore, but I also knew he was big enough that Dad wouldn't kill him. So, I put him back with the other pigs. He was still my pet though, and whenever I would go out to the barn he'd come running over to me. I'd sit beside him, talk to him about my problems, and scratch him behind his ears, and he'd stick his muzzle into my face, grunting his approval.

About a year later, I was sitting at the table one morning eating breakfast when I heard Dad say he was going to shoot Scottie. I couldn't believe what I was hearing! He couldn't shoot Scottie! Scottie was my pet, my friend! But Dad grabbed his .22 and headed out to the barn, and I followed behind him in a state of shock. I wanted to say or do something, but I didn't know what I could do. Instead, I just stood there and watched as Dad put a rope around Scottie's neck and got one of my brothers to hold him. Scottie didn't know what was going on, and he was so tame that he let Dad walk right up to him and put the barrel of the gun between his eyes. I don't know what Dad was thinking, trying to shoot him there, because a bullet will just deflect off a pig's forehead. But he put the barrel up against Scottie's head and pulled the trigger.

Scottie went ballistic. He started squealing and running around, and my brother could barely hold the rope. Dad sent one of my other brothers into the house for more bullets, but he came back a couple of minutes later, saying that he couldn't find any. Blood was running down Scottie's face, and he kept looking at me, screaming and squealing. Finally they managed to get another rope around his head so they could hold him still, and Dad went up to him and cut his throat.

Tears were streaming down my face. I had just lost my best friend. It was a grey, cloudy day outside, and that's how I was feeling on the inside, too. I moped around for weeks afterwards, feeling lonely and depressed, but mostly feeling guilty and ashamed. I felt like I had killed Scottie myself because I hadn't done anything to stop it. I was mad, and I knew that one day I would pay Dad back for what he had done.

Dad was a fighter, and he was brutally violent. He was just a small man, but he was unbelievably tough. He and Carol often had friends over, and they would drink together late into the night. Quite often fights would break out between Dad and whoever was over. I don't know what they fought about, and I don't think they always knew either, but they didn't really need a reason to fight. They'd just start arguing and yelling, and soon fists would be flying. Dad loved to fight; he loved the violence. In the morning we kids would go downstairs and see them passed out and lying around on the floor. Drinking, drugs, sex and violence were constant activities in our house. Very little effort was made to hide any of it from us.

The fights between my sister Maureen and Carol were some of the fiercest battles I can ever remember seeing. Maureen was ten years younger than Carol, but like our dad, she was tough. Dad started sleeping with Maureen shortly after we arrived. She was only 14 years old, but she was very pretty and could easily pass for being a few years older. He had no trouble taking her out to the pool halls and bars where he spent his time. He would get her drunk and then keep her out all night. After a while she was so messed up by the alcohol and sexual abuse that she started to see herself more as a wife than a daughter. This led to some bitter fights between her and Carol. Dad would sometimes have to get off his tractor in the field and come to the house to separate them. It's a wonder they didn't kill each other.

It sounds screwed up, but that's what we were—a screwed-up family. We were growing up in a culture of violence, drugs, alcohol and sexual abuse. It was all we knew.

Rena was the "mom" of the family. She was only 11, but she was the one who got us off to school in the mornings, did the laundry, and made the meals. Anything that in any way resembled a normal family in our house was because of her. At Christmas that first year, she went out with Dad to buy presents for all of us. There wasn't much money to spend because Dad and Carol drank it all away, but she tried so hard to surprise everyone with something special.

Dad wasn't very often physically abusive to us kids. When he was in a rage he didn't know how to hold back, and if that rage would have been turned towards us I have no doubt that someone would have died. But although he didn't beat us physically, he was horribly sexually abusive. He had sex with the girls, and he touched and fondled us boys, too. I hated him for it.

Early one morning just as the sun was rising, I woke up to the sound of Rena crying and screaming. I ran into her room to see what was wrong, and saw Dad lying on top of her on her bed. She was struggling and crying, so I started pulling his hair and yelling, trying to get him off. He turned around and hit me in the face, sending me sprawling onto the floor. I crawled over to the edge of the bed and held Rena's hand while this drunken pig who was our father raped her. The blood dripping from my nose and the tears running down my cheeks pooled together on the floor as Rena and I held hands and sobbed.

A couple of days later I heard her go downstairs early in the morning. I followed and found her sitting in our big, black rocking chair. She was curled up in a tight little ball, slowly rocking back and forth, and crying. I climbed up beside her and we rocked and cried together. From that day on, we got up together every morning to sit in the big chair and rock and cry until it was time for her to get the other kids up and put breakfast on the table.

At school I pretty much kept to myself, and hardly ever said a word to anyone. At recess one day I was watching a group of kids playing baseball and it looked like they were having so much fun that I worked up the courage to go ask if I could play, too. They told me I couldn't, so I just stood off to the side and watched. After recess was over I was walking back to class, minding my own business, when the kid who had told me I couldn't play ran up beside me. I thought he was going to just keep going, but he turned around and kicked me in the groin so hard that I crumpled to the ground and started to throw up. He was a year or two older and a lot bigger than me—he hurt me really bad. I stayed there moaning on the ground until a teacher came out to help me into the school. I was so sick that I got sent home and didn't go back to school for a few more days.

When my dad found out what had happened, he told me I needed to fight back. He said that if I didn't beat the crap out of the kid who did this to me, then he would beat the crap out of me himself.

On my first day back at school I walked into the boy's washroom and there was the kid who had kicked me, standing with his back to me at the urinal. I wasn't looking for him; I was actually trying to avoid him. I had only gone in there because I was so terrified of running into him that I had to pee. But when I saw him standing there, something inside me snapped. It felt like a switch had been turned on and I lost control. It had never happened before, but suddenly all of the hurt and rage bottled up inside of me took over.

He didn't realize I was behind him, and he never saw me coming. I ran across the room and drove him face first into the urinal. Before he could recover, I grabbed him by the hair and started smashing his head against the wall. Then I pulled him into one of the stalls and flushed his head in the toilet, just like Doris had done to me so often. I finally dragged him over to the trash can and started stuffing him headfirst through the flip-top lid. The sharp, metal edges on the lid ripped up and gouged his face. A bunch of other kids came rushing in when they heard all the commotion. They were crying and screaming and telling me to stop, but I kept yelling and tearing up his face, until a teacher finally came and pulled me off.

It was the first time I had felt that kind of insatiable rage, like the way a pressure cooker keeps building up pressure until it gets so high that it blows the valve open. There's no way you can stop it—it can't be held inside anymore. When the explosion of rage finally comes, it's ugly and destructive.

I had always defended myself as best as I could from Doris, and I had been in a few fights with other kids, but I had never lashed out with that kind of fury. It surprised me, and I started to realize that day that I had a special gift. It didn't matter how big or how mean anyone was; if I could tap into the rage inside of me I could destroy anyone. I didn't have to run and hide anymore. I could fight back—I would fight back.

I never saw that kid again. I don't know what happened to him, but he never came back to school after that.

A couple of weeks later a school counselor came to our house to talk to Dad and Carol. I stood in the next room and listened. I heard the counselor say she thought I might have mental problems. I already wasn't talking either at home or at school unless I absolutely had to, and after seeing how I had attacked that boy, they were beginning to wonder if something was mentally wrong with me.

Beating up the bully didn't just get me into trouble—it also made me a new friend. George was a fat kid who rode the same school bus as me. Like me, he was always being picked on at school, so after I took out the bully he started to hang around with me. It was good to have someone to talk to and hang around with. Over the next few weeks the other kids learned to leave us alone. Any time someone picked on George, I stepped in and took care of it. No one wanted to mess with me—they were scared of me. I liked it that way. I felt safe.

Unfortunately, my friendship with George didn't last all that long. Our school had a milk program where each student brought 45 cents a week to pay for a daily carton of milk. I couldn't help but notice that when the teacher collected the money, she put it into a small box inside her desk drawer. After thinking this over for a day or two, I decided I had more use for the money than she did. So, one afternoon when no one was around, I snuck over to her desk and helped myself. After school, George and I split the loot—$15 in cold, hard change. I went to the store on my way home and bought a box of Cap'n Crunch cereal. I ate the whole thing while I was walking home.

The next morning when George got on the bus I could tell right away that something wasn't right. I was sitting in my usual spot near the back, but instead of coming to join me, George stayed up at the front and sat right behind the driver. He wouldn't even look in my direction.

I found out later that his mother had caught him with a bulging pocketful of change. Under interrogation he had come clean and told her everything. She sent him back to school with the money and a note, explaining that the whole scheme had been conceived, planned and carried out by me alone. I had been ratted out!

When school started that morning, the teacher stood at the front of the class and explained that someone had stolen the milk money, and asked for that person to come forward. I looked over at George to see what he might be thinking, but he still wasn't looking at me. It was obvious he wasn't going to the front, and I sure as heck wasn't! The teacher asked a few more times, and when no one moved from their desk, she called my name. "Richard, would you come up here, please?" she asked.

I stood up and walked to the front. "Richard, I know you took the money," she said, "so I think it would be best if you would just admit it."

I didn't feel like admitting anything. I figured confessing would get me into more trouble than I was already in, so I kept my mouth shut. She kept talking to me but I just stared straight ahead like she wasn't even there. The longer I ignored her, the more she raised her voice. After a while she got really mad and slapped me in the face. She said again, "I know you took the money, so just admit it!"

This went on for a few minutes as she got angrier and louder all the time. She started to yell and hit me even harder, but I still didn't even flinch. A little red-haired girl in the front row started to cry, and I could see that some of the other kids were getting scared.

She told me to hold out my hands. I did, and then she picked up a wooden yardstick and hit me with it. I just went on staring straight ahead, ignoring her. This was nothing; I had been beaten a lot worse than this, more times than I could count. She hit me a few more times on my hands and then finally lost it, hitting me across my back so hard that the yardstick snapped in half. Another one of the girls started crying and ran out of the room. The teacher just stood there, shaking. She didn't know what to do. She stood there hyperventilating and vibrating. She had done everything she could to break me, but instead, I had broken her. We stood there for a minute or so more and then another teacher came into the classroom and took the broken stick from her hand. I went back to sit at my desk, feeling quite proud of myself. I never did confess to taking that money.

That day was another turning point in my life. I realized that my ability to withstand pain was a powerful tool. As long as they didn't know they were hurting me—as long as they couldn't break me—I had power over them.

The other kids at school all left me alone after that. They were afraid of me, and looked at me like I was some kind of a freak. My only friend at school was my sister, Rena.

It was around this time that I started drinking alcohol quite heavily, for a kid. There were always half-full glasses of booze around our house, so I had already been helping myself, and getting drunk quite a few times. But now I began to drink whenever I could. When Rena and I got up in the mornings I would go around the house with an empty Cheez Whiz jar, collecting beer, rye, rum, wine, or whatever drink I could find leftover from the night before. Sometimes I would mix them because I thought the colors looked pretty. I would fill up my jar and take it to school with me in a paper bag. Other kids brought a lunch to school. My lunch included my Cheez Whiz jar full of booze.

I drank before school, during recess and at lunch. There was never any left by the time the afternoon recess came around. At nine years old I was drinking to escape the pain. I felt pain on every level—physical, emotional and mental. It all hurt. I couldn't make heads nor tails out of life, so I drank to escape it for a while.

One day at school I touched a girl sexually. I think it was the first time I had ever done anything like that. I had been on the receiving end of a lot of physical, and sometimes sexual, abuse, but up until then I had never been the one to initiate it. I'm not sure why I did it, but to me it was really no big deal. It was just something that happened all the time in my world.

My teacher phoned home and told Carol what I had done, so when I walked into the house that afternoon she was waiting for me. I took one look at her and knew I was in trouble. She grabbed me by the ear, dragged me into the bathroom and started yelling and slapping me around. When Maureen heard what was going on, she kicked in the bathroom door, and then she and Carol started going at it. I ducked out of the way and got out of there as fast as I could. I heard the mirror smash to pieces behind me. By the time they were done, the room was a mess—broken glass, blood and fistfuls of hair everywhere.

The next day was Saturday, and I spent the day putting together a plan. I decided I would run away. I would take whatever I needed and just disappear. I was scared, confused, and tired of being hurt. I didn't want to be part of a family anymore, so I would just go away and make it on my own.

The next morning I got up early while everyone was still sleeping, and put on several layers of clothes. I didn't want to carry a bag, and I figured that was the best way to bring my clothes with me. I grabbed a loaf of bread and a jar of raspberry jam from the kitchen. I quietly snuck my dad's old Cooey .22 and a box of 50 shells. Then I woke up Rena to say goodbye, and quietly slipped out the door.

I started heading down the road without knowing where I was going. I just knew I was going away, and no one was ever going to touch me again. I was tired of the pain, and I was ready to shoot the next person who tried to lay a hand on me.

I went a couple of miles down the road and then headed off into the middle of a cornfield and sat down. After a while I started to get hungry, so I opened up the jar of jam and took out a few slices of bread. The jam was runny, so I just poured some of it onto the bread and ate it. I was still hungry, so I ate some more slices and then decided I should save some of my food. I closed the lid and tucked the jar beside me.

I spent the whole day in that cornfield. I really didn't know where to go or what to do, so I just sat there. Towards evening a small bird landed on a cornstalk not too far away. After watching it for a while I decided that if I was going to live off the land I was going to need more food. The bird wasn't much I figured, but it was a start. I took three shots at it before it flew away.

About half an hour later I heard some vehicles driving close by. Someone had reported hearing gunshots, and after a short investigation (the police knew exactly which house to go to) they discovered I was missing, and so was a gun. They started calling to me from the edge of the field. "Rocky, come out here, please. We just want to talk to you. We won't hurt you." They were trying to sound friendly, but there was no way I was coming out! I wasn't going back home. No one was going to hurt me again!

When the sun went down and it started getting dark, I started to feel very alone and afraid. I was scared and crying, but I still had 47 shots left, and I was ready to defend myself to the end, whatever that would mean. I stayed awake all night and shot in the direction of every sound I heard. I heard a lot of noises that night, so I did quite a bit of shooting. The police kept calling out to me every so often through their megaphone. My only response was an occasional shot fired in their general direction. When the sun came up the next morning I only had three bullets left. They kept talking to me and asking me to come out, but I wasn't moving.

I knew I was going to have a problem later that day when I poured out the last bit of jam, but still I wasn't giving up. I would stay and fight until the end. Sometime that afternoon I finally fell asleep. I must have really been tired, because I didn't even notice when the policeman walked over and picked me up. I just woke up as he was carrying me out of the field.

They took me home, and my dad, who had been drinking as usual, yelled at me to get upstairs. It was obvious to the policeman that this wasn't going to end well for me, so he got into Dad's face and did a little threatening of his own. He told Dad to feed me something, and then stood there and watched as I ate a big bowl of stew. After spending two cold days and a night out in a cornfield, that stew sure tasted good.

Before the policeman left, he threatened Dad again and told him that he'd better start looking after me. He said that he'd be coming around to check on me, so things had better change! He came back a few days later just like he promised, and brought me a box of Fig Newton cookies. I kept them hidden and ate them all myself. The next time he came around, he and Dad had some pretty harsh words. I don't remember exactly what they were arguing about, but it must have been clear to him that we weren't being looked after very well.

My second attempt at running away came about a month later. Ray said that if I really wanted to run away he would come with me. He told me he knew how to hot-wire a car, so we'd really be able to get away. That sounded good to me.

Early the next Saturday morning we packed a few clothes, grabbed some food, and hit the road. We were living quite far out in the county, about five miles from the closest town. When we got there we looked around for a while until Ray finally saw a car he thought he could steal. He told me to hide in the ditch with our bags while he ran across the road. The plan was for me to stay hidden until he got the car out to the road. Then I'd jump in and we'd take off. It seemed like the plan should work.

Our timing couldn't have been worse. Ray had just snuck into the back seat when the owner came out of the house. He didn't realize Ray was there, so he just jumped into his car and started to leave. As he was backing out of his driveway he saw Ray crouched down behind the seat. I watched from across the road as the owner slammed on the brakes, jumped out of the car and grabbed Ray, who wasn't much bigger than me, by the back of his shirt and carried him, kicking and screaming, into the house.

I had no idea what was going to happen next, so I decided to grab our stuff and move to a different spot further along the ditch, just in case they came looking for me, too. Ray must have started talking, because a minute or two later the curtains parted a little bit and I saw them looking across the road, pointing to where I had been hiding. I kept watching, and a couple of minutes later the curtains opened all the way. There was Ray, sitting in a big chair by the window drinking hot chocolate and eating cookies. I couldn't believe it! He was looking out the window, smiling and stuffing his face with cookies!

I sat there watching until I couldn't take it any more, and went over and knocked on the door. When the owner answered, I told him I was Ray's brother. "Can I have some cookies, too?" I asked. He invited me in, poured me a big mug of hot chocolate and then brought out some more cookies. He was one of the nicest people I had ever met. I remember wondering what he thought of these two scrawny kids trying to steal his car. I also remember wishing he was my dad.

After a while he called the police, who picked us up again and brought us back to the last place we wanted to be—home.

We got whipped pretty badly after the police left, and I think that time Ray took the brunt of it. A few days later when Dad and Carol went into town, Ray decided to get them back. He wasn't much of a fighter, but he acted out his rage in other ways. There was always lots of collateral damage when Ray was upset about something, which was almost always. After Dad and Carol left, Rena, Larry and I went to the store to buy some

Mojos. When we got back home, Ray's work was already done. He had buried Carol's cat in the ground with just its head sticking out and then ran over it with the lawn mower. Then he found the keys to Dad's truck, and drove it into the lake.

Shortly after that, Ray was sent to a detention home in London, Ont., but even there they couldn't control him—he kept escaping. Once when he was out, he stole a car, lit it on fire and rolled it down a hill in the middle of town. Everything for him needed to be ugly and violent. It didn't matter what was going on—Ray was always swinging with all he had.

He had it rough. We all had it rough.

CHAPTER 3

I was beginning to think that maybe I really was mentally retarded. After all, I'd sure heard it often enough. Several times I overheard my teachers telling Dad and Carol that I had severe problems. One day I heard them talking about my sister Carol, who was locked away in an institution. I had heard bits and pieces of information about her before, but it seemed to me that no one really wanted to talk about her. She was like some sort of family secret. All I knew was that she was the oldest of the kids and that something had happened to her when Doris was pregnant with me. No one ever came right out and said it, but I had the impression that Doris had beaten her pretty badly. Carol had been locked up in a mental institution since then. When I heard them comparing me to her, I started wondering if they wanted to lock me away, too. It was becoming clear to me I was just a problem, and that no one wanted me around.

About this time, our family started to get split apart again. Social Services was becoming more involved again, and there was talk that some of us would be leaving. We heard that some of us might even be sent back to live with Al and Doris. Ray was already off in a juvenile detention home in London, Ont.. Then Maureen left home. I'm not sure where she went, but one day she was just gone, and I didn't see her again for a long time. It was all very unsettling for me. As fragile as my world was, my older brothers and sisters had always been there, and to see the family starting to disintegrate made me afraid.

One day Carol showed me and Rena how to use a Ouija board. We spent hours on it, trying to get answers to the questions that were weighing on our minds. When would we be split up? Would we see each other again? Would the other brothers and sisters make it? Where would we go? When would we die? Those aren't the kinds of questions that kids should have to ask, but those were the questions that plagued us.

When we asked the Ouija board to tell us when I would die, it answered that my death would be in the month of July when I was thirty-five years old. That answer was confirmed at least six or seven times over the years by tarot cards, palm readers, tea leaf readers and other mediums that I consulted. I was convinced that the Ouija board had not lied.

Again I was struggling in school. It's not that I wasn't smart enough—I actually understood what was being taught quite well. But with everything else going on in my life, my schoolwork suffered. Also, because I never talked unless I absolutely had to, my teachers thought there was something wrong with me. My schoolwork wasn't up to standard, but the teachers passed me anyway. They either felt sorry for me or just didn't want to deal with me anymore.

At Easter break that year my brothers and sisters who were still at home all got taken away and sent to live in other homes.

They were taken by people who knew us and just wanted to help. Doris wanted Larry to live with her, and the other kids were chosen by other families, but no one wanted me. Again, I understood clearly that I was unwanted.

Eventually I was told I would be going back to live with Doris, and I remember hoping I wouldn't get killed. I decided to keep my mouth shut and try to not make her mad, but I was so afraid for my life, and started thinking about how I would get away and where I would go if I needed to run.

Doris came to Brantford, Ont. to pick us up and then rode the train with us back to Thunder Bay where she was living. On the train she told us she had gotten healthier and things would be different now, but I didn't believe a word she said. I just hoped that the new power I had discovered inside me would be enough to get me through what I knew was coming.

The house we moved into was the worst place I had ever lived in. We had certainly lived in some dumps, but this was the worst. It was a tiny, rundown shack, with a total of maybe 500 square feet of living space. It was so crowded inside that we had to keep the fridge out on the porch. The house was located between the train tracks and the docks, right next to where the city's sewer came out. The whole area had been condemned, and everyone else who had been living there had already moved away. Ours was the only occupied house left in the neighbourhood.

From the day we got back things turned ugly, with the old pattern of abuse picking up right where it had left off. If there had been any change in Doris it was a change for the worse—she was now even more violent than I remembered. Larry was the youngest of her boys, and clearly her favourite. But as much as she favoured him, it seemed like she despised me ten times more. Any time he cried, got hurt or implicated me in anything, I got a beating for it. Larry played on that whenever he could. He was so starved for any kind of attention that he would tell her about every little thing I did wrong, and when I hadn't done anything wrong he would make something up. I think he wanted Doris's approval, and that was the one way he was sure to get it. We all needed to find our own way of surviving. That was his. Seeing me get a beating made him feel better about himself.

I felt sorry for him, but I also started to hate him for what he was doing to me. He wasn't a brother anymore, just like Doris wasn't my mother.

One day, while he was playing with a toy car he got a tiny cut on the tip of his finger. He looked over at me, held up his finger and said, "I'm going to tell Mom you cut my finger, and you're going to get it." He was right. Doris grabbed me by the hair and dragged me across the living room floor, through the kitchen and into the bathroom. The whole way she was hitting me with her free hand and yelling that she was going to kill me. I had heard that so many times already that I should have been used to it, but every time she said it I still feared for my life. I was afraid that one of these times she really would follow through on her threat. She was vicious.

She dragged me into bathroom and kept yelling over and over, "I hate you! I hate you!" while she slammed my head against the side of the toilet bowl. I remember seeing the water in the bowl turn red and then tasting my own blood and starting to choke as she pushed my face down into the toilet. I was drowning.

I woke up on the floor later that day with my head pounding. There was a pool of blood on the floor where she had left me after I passed out.

I know Doris realized that Larry wasn't always telling the truth, but it was like she couldn't help herself, or didn't want to. She would turn on me at the slightest provocation. I sometimes wonder about the kind of ugliness she had gone through that had poisoned her and turned her into such an angry, hateful person.

On my 13th birthday I decided to go for a walk down by the docks. I knew that nothing would be made of my birthday at home, so I thought I'd just spend the day at the waterfront. While I was wandering around I met another boy about my age. We spent the afternoon goofing around and throwing rocks at the ships out in the harbour. When I got home I stepped inside the door and told Doris I had made a new friend, and I was going over to his place to play. She instantly turned on me. She hit me five or six times and then threw me against the door frame. I hit my head hard and then stumbled backwards and fell against the fridge. I was sitting there dazed with the back of my head against the fridge when she kicked me right in the face. The only thing that could give was my nose. I felt the bones crack, and instantly the blood was pouring down my face. It was just another typical day in my world. "Happy Birthday, Richard," I whispered to myself.

When I went to school that fall I again tried to stay as quiet and invisible as possible. I had to ride the city bus to get to school, which was a new experience for me. I was a little bit intimidated at first, but after a while it was no big deal. I just kept to myself and didn't speak to anyone.

At lunch one day I was sitting on the grass watching some kids play basketball. It was an open court with the ground banked up all around. I was just sitting there by myself watching the other kids playing when the ball came bouncing up close to me. It rolled over beside me, and this jock named Eugene came to get it. I didn't bother looking up because I didn't want to get involved in anything. He picked up the ball, but then instead of bringing it back to the court, he bounced it off my forehead. The other kids all started laughing and thinking it was a big joke. I felt the rage building up inside of me, and instantly I recognized it. It was the same rage that had taken over when I had beaten up the school bully in the bathroom. The switch had been turned on, and I knew that Eugene was in trouble.

I was scared to go to school the next day, but not for myself—I was scared for Eugene. I knew that things were going to get ugly and that he was going to get hurt badly. Before I left for school that morning I went into the kitchen and stuck a paring knife into my pocket.

At lunchtime I slid the knife up my sleeve and then went out to the basketball court and sat in the exact same spot and waited. When the ball came close to where I was sitting, Eugene again came over and threw it at me, just like I knew he would. I was ready this time, and I caught the ball and held it in my lap. He told me to give it back, and I ignored him. He called me a few names and again told me to give him the ball, but I just kept ignoring him. The other kids were all watching to see what would happen. He finally came over and reached for the ball, and when he did I grabbed him by the hair, spun him down to the ground and held the knife against his throat. I was vibrating with rage, and I could see the fear in his eyes. I stared him right in the face and said, "If you ever touch me again, I will kill you." We were both vibrating, me with anger and him with fear.

The next thing I knew, I had been clocked in the side of the head and was sprawled out on the ground. The teacher who was outside on supervision duty had seen what was going on and had come to Eugene's rescue. He brought me into the office where the school principal told me he would be calling my mom to tell her what had happened. I just sat there quietly and didn't say anything.

I knew that when I got home I was going to get it, so I figured I might as well finish this up with Eugene while I had the chance. My bus stop was the one after his, but I got off that afternoon at the same place as he did. We had just stepped off the bus and onto the sidewalk when he looked at me and said, "You're not so tough now without your knife, are you?" I was just a scrawny little kid, and he was a lot bigger and tougher looking than I was, but that insatiable rage inside of me again took over. He took a couple of steps towards me and I flew into him. He was so surprised that I don't think he even got in one shot. I knocked him over and probably punched him 15 or 20 times in the face before the bus driver managed to get over there and pull me off of him. My fists were flying, and his face was taking a serious pounding. It's a good thing the bus driver got there when he did, because I still had lots of energy and plenty of rage inside of me, and I was just getting going.

I walked home knowing that I was in for a beating, but feeling good because of what I had done to Eugene. The thrashing from Doris was more of the same—I was nothing but a piece of garbage, and she wished I was dead.

After a few more months of living there, my brothers and sisters started showing up and moving in with us. I'm not sure why, or what was going on with Social Services, but suddenly we were all together again. Ray either got out or broke out of reform school. He was in and out a lot over the next few years. Then Maureen came back from wherever she had gone, and the other kids came over from the families that they had been living with. The only one who didn't move in with us was Guy. Suddenly there were six kids and one very angry woman living in a tiny, rundown house on the wrong side of the tracks. Maureen and Doris were like a couple of gladiators going at it constantly. Maureen stayed for just a couple of months and then left again. The circus came through town, and when it packed up to go, she went with it. She ended up marrying a carnie named John. They're still married today.

One morning I found $20 lying on the sidewalk as I was going over to a friend's house to walk to school together. My friend was another kid who was being picked on at school, and we had started chumming around after I beat up Eugene. We went to the store and spent half the money on candy. Ten dollars bought a lot of candy back then, so we had a huge bag filled with penny and 5-cent candies. I brought the bag to school and handed out some of the candy to the people that I liked. I liked the feeling of power it gave me. I ate a lot of candy that day, so I wasn't very hungry when I got home.

There was never much money in our house, so I tried to be nice by giving Doris the $10 that I had left over. I told her I had found it, but she accused me of stealing it from her purse, and she beat me for it. It was a bad beating, worse than usual.

My brother Ray was stealing money from Doris, and so was Al, whenever he was around, but I never once stole from her. Even so, I still got blamed whenever money went missing. There were times when I knew that money had been taken from her purse, so I would get some money from somewhere and replace what had been taken just so I wouldn't get beaten. I probably put money into her purse six or eight times over the years, but I never once stole from her.

A few days after the incident with the $20, I went for a walk with Rena to the library. She had some overdue books, but when she went up to the desk and explained why she hadn't been able to come in and return them on time the lady waived the late fee. That gave me an idea, and I decided right then to get a library card and take out some books. I kept the books until they were overdue and then started approaching people on the street within a block or two of the library. I would show them my overdue books and ask if they had any spare change to help me out, because I didn't have any money for the late fees. People felt sorry for me and would give me a quarter or sometimes 50 cents. It worked quite well, and it became a steady source of income for me for the next several months. I avoided people that I thought looked mean or those I had approached with the same scam before. I used the money to buy candy or to replace the money that Ray was stealing from Doris' purse.

Ray didn't know how to stay out of trouble. One day while he was out he witnessed a local biker gang kill someone. He tried to slip away unnoticed, but they saw him. He had been hanging around the pool hall, and one of the bikers recognized him. A few days later about a dozen bikers came roaring up to our place on their choppers. Doris went out and talked to them while we watched from the front of the house. I have no idea what she said, but there was some finger pointing and yelling and a few glances thrown in our direction. Then the bikers rode off. For all we knew she told them she'd kill us herself if we ever talked. Whatever she said seemed to satisfy them, because they never hassled us again. She was one scary lady.

That was my first look at a biker gang, and I liked what I saw. Later that summer I climbed a tree so I could watch a war between them and another rival gang. I was in awe of the violence. They were going at it with chains, clubs, knives and bare fists. They were warriors. I was impressed.

That summer we finally moved out of the squalor we were living in. The city opened up a huge townhouse complex for low income families like ours. There were hundreds of us living in close quarters, and quite a few of us were from troubled and dysfunctional homes. To say that it got fairly chaotic at times wouldn't be an exaggeration. It was a rough place, and the police were always coming around for some reason or another.

In one of the neighbouring units there was a family with two older boys. I started calling one of them "Tarzan" for no reason other than I knew he didn't like it. He would then grab me and beat me up, but I really didn't mind. Beatings were such a normal part of my life that it almost didn't bother me anymore. Besides, I told him that my big brothers were going to pound on him. When Guy moved in with us a little while later that's exactly what happened. They beat up the neighbour boys pretty badly. Tarzan didn't bother me anymore after that.

That winter a few of us joined a local rec-hockey league. We played on an outdoor rink and sometimes the games got pretty rough, but I liked it that way. Guy was an amazing hockey player, and he was our coach. His foster family had put him in a hockey program, and he was a really good player. One day one of the boys on the team we were playing against was getting a little out of control and taking a few cheap shots at the guys on our team. He was also their best player and had already scored a couple of goals. About halfway through the game Guy called me over and told me to not let that kid get past. I knew what that meant, or at least I thought I did. On the next rush he came skating down my wing and gave me a bit of a butt end with his stick as he went by. I turned around and gave him a full, two-handed swing with my stick right in the side of his head. I knocked him out cold. I felt pretty good for stopping him, but Guy told me to take off my skates and go home. That was the end of my hockey career.

When spring rolled around Guy and Ray decided they were going to leave home. They told Doris they were going to hitchhike to B.C. It sounded like a good plan to me, so I announced that I would be going with them. Doris flew into a rage, grabbed me by the neck and started choking me. I remember seeing Rena crying, and feeling Doris's fingernails digging into my neck. I could taste my own blood, and then everything went into slow motion and faded to black.

I found out later that Ray had come to my defense and knocked her out with a cast iron frying pan. While she was lying there on the floor Guy and Ray packed up a few things and left. That was the end of them in my life. I wouldn't hear from either of them again for many years.

When Doris woke up, she came at me with a fury like I had never seen before. I honestly thought she was going to kill me right there. Ray had left his guitar behind, and since it was the handiest thing within reach she picked it up and started hitting me with it. She smashed it to pieces on me and then finally hit me over the head so hard that she knocked me out. I was beat unconscious twice that day.

We finished that school year and then left Thunder Bay and moved back to Prince George. Al had been working there in the bush and Doris decided that we would go to join him.

The school year was just coming to an end when we got there, and the local elementary school was having a year-end dance. Larry and I decided this would be a good chance to get to know some new people and maybe hook up with some girls. Even though I was always getting picked on and beaten up, I still had a lot of self-confidence, especially around girls. I liked girls. I also liked music and I was a good dancer, so I was looking forward to the dance. When we got there Larry was allowed in because he would be attending the school in the fall. But the school principal told me that since I would be going into Junior High he saw no reason for me to attend the dance.

I told him I had no place to go because we had been dropped off and I didn't have a ride back home. "That's not my problem," he said, and then shut the door in my face.

I had nothing to do, so I just went and sat on the hood of a car in the parking lot. A few minutes later he stuck his head out the door and yelled at me to get off his car. I hadn't realized it was his car, but I complied with his request and got off. When he went back inside I pulled out my knife and slashed his tires. I had been carrying a knife ever since the fight with Eugene, and I figured that was as good a use as any for it.

I then decided that it might be advantageous for me to walk home after all. As I was nearing our house I heard a car coming up behind me, so I hid in the ditch. It was a police car, and I naturally assumed it was heading for our place, so I took my time getting home. They were long gone by the time I walked in the door, but Doris had been filled in and she was waiting for me. That was one of the few beatings I think I actually might have deserved.

Al decided we needed a more permanent place to live, so he bought a small plot of land in the bush, 25 miles from the city. We spent the next couple of weeks clearing an area of trees and stumps, and then had a house trailer moved in. For the first while there were no services or plumbing, so one of my daily chores was to empty the sewer buckets. Doris would sometimes trip me or knock me over while I was carrying them out, and then swear at me and make me clean up the mess.

She was becoming more cruel and sadistic all the time. Once again she started calling me "the dog". I never knew what I was being beaten for; sometimes the smallest thing would set her off. Other times I wouldn't do or say anything and she would just come at me.

Al and I had dug a cellar beneath the trailer. It was just an open pit with a trap door on top and a ladder staircase leading down to the dirt floor. After beating me Doris would sometimes throw me down the stairs and slam the door. I didn't dare come back out because I knew what would be waiting for me if I did. On more than one occasion I spent a night down there. I got quite familiar with the dirt floor, the musty smell and the resident mice.

The only light coming into the cellar was from a tiny crack around the door, so I would crawl to the top of the ladder and lie there with my head against the little opening. I was sleeping there once when I suddenly realized that the door had been opened. I looked up just as Doris' foot stomped onto my face. I woke up some time later with blood and dirt caked on my face and mice running around on my head. I just lay there and screamed so long and so hard that after a while I could hear someone screaming, but it was like it wasn't really me. I screamed until I was so exhausted that I passed out again.

After we'd been living in the country for a couple of months a guy from a few miles down the road came over one day and told us that the Baptist church he attended in Prince George had a really good youth program. He said that if any of us kids were interested he would pick us up and bring us to the Friday evening events. The only time I'd been to church was back in Upsala when I was six or seven years old. A neighbour had brought us to the Catholic church for Mass a few times. I hadn't liked anything about it. I didn't like the smell of the incense, I didn't like the taste of that dry wafer they put on your tongue and I didn't like the way everyone had to drink out of the same cup. Actually, you couldn't even take a real drink; you were just supposed to let your lips touch the juice. That didn't make any sense to me. But I especially didn't like the way we had to kneel at the front of the church. Kneeling was a submissive position, and I didn't kneel to anyone.

In spite of my negative memories from church I decided I would give this youth group a try. I went a few times, but it really wasn't my thing. The kids seemed nice enough, but I couldn't relate to them. Their world was completely different than mine. They were talking about a God I knew nothing about.

That fall I started attending grade seven at Blackburn Jr. High. Right away I was back into the old cycle of fighting and violence, but I didn't try to avoid it this time. In fact, I went looking for it. Fighting was all I knew. The older kids just treated me like a punching bag. I had never been treated well at school, but that year was the worst. There was never a time during that fall that I wasn't covered with bruises. I was fighting back, but it was always groups of kids that I was up against, and they were always older and bigger. It was like a game to them. They'd egg me on, and when I fought back they'd beat me up.

Me in Grade 7

We all had to go to the lunch room at noon to eat our lunch. Very often I didn't eat anything; I preferred a liquid lunch. I would just sit there by myself sipping from my jar of booze. One day, while I was sitting there a guy named Bobby came up to me. He was a big, strong farm kid that everybody liked—kind of a gentle giant. "Here," he said, sliding a bag lunch over to me. "My mom packed some extra sandwiches and stuff."

From then on he started sticking up for me and we became pretty good friends. He was a really good kid with a big heart. He felt sorry for me and tried to get me to not drink and fight so much. He was a true friend who wanted a better life for me.

I also had a couple of really good teachers who genuinely cared about me and tried to help as best they could. The only class I was passing or that I even showed up for regularly was English. The teacher, Mrs. Fraser, took the time to encourage me and to talk to me not just about school, but also about other things that were going on in my life. I felt that she was someone who truly cared.

Mrs. Rowe was the librarian. She was a tiny lady who was in her last year before retirement. She was so kind and gentle to me that I thought of her as an angel. She told me I was the reason she was still at school. She could see that my life was quickly going from bad to worse and that if things didn't change I probably wasn't going to make it.

I had told her a bit of my story, so she knew that my dad lived in Ontario. One day that spring she helped me get in touch with him on the school phone. I talked to him for a while and told him that things were really bad and that I wanted to go back and live with him. He said that he and Carol were planning on taking a trip out west that summer, and that along the way he would stop in and get me. That, at least, gave me a reason to hang on. I don't know what I would have done without Mrs. Rowe.

I had already been through hell living with my dad, so I knew it wouldn't be easy going back, but I was desperate. I had to do something. I thought that maybe my chances would be better with him. I was bigger now, so maybe I could defend myself. I didn't know, but I couldn't go on any longer the way things were.

The next few weeks were just a blur of fights at school and beatings at home. One day Doris threw me right through the closet doors at the end of the hall. The broken closet doors seemed to send her into even more of a rage, and she started kicking and stomping on me while she braced herself by hanging on to the coat rack. The metal bar eventually came loose in her hands and she started hitting me with it. I put up my hands to protect my head, but she just kept on swinging, hitting me over and over again. She was swinging hard, and as the bar smashed repeatedly onto the top of my shoulders I felt both of my collarbones break. With my collarbones broken I couldn't hold my arms up, but she didn't show any mercy—I don't think she knew what mercy was. She just kept on hitting me, and I started to think that maybe this time she wouldn't stop until it was too late. I just lay there on the floor and she hit me over and over. It was one of the worst beatings I ever had.

She ended up splitting my head open and breaking my collarbones so badly that they never did heal properly and are deformed to this day.

After that beating I realized it was only a matter of time until she killed me. I knew that if I didn't get out of there I would die. I couldn't wait for summer when my dad would come get me. I had to run.

CHAPTER 4

After a couple of weeks I had healed up enough that I told Doris I was going back to school. I then walked the 2½ miles to the junction at Highway 16 and started hitchhiking south to Vancouver. A guy named Roland that I had gotten to know from school came along with me. He was a tall, skinny kid who came from a well-to-do home. Earlier on I had told him that I had run away a few times before, and he told me then that when I took off the next time, he wanted to come along. I thought it might be nice to have some company, and he also said he could bring $50. That sounded alright to me.

That morning I tried to phone him several times, but the party line we were on was busy whenever I tried to get through. If we were going to go that day I had to get ahold of him before he left for school, so finally I called the operator and told her, in the most desperate voice I could muster up, that there was an emergency and I needed her to put me through right away. She wanted to know what the emergency was, so I quickly made something up. I told her that a buddy of mine was planning to buy a horse but the owner was going to shoot it that day if he didn't show up with the money. She told me to calm down and assured me that no horse was going to get shot if she had anything to do with it. She then patched me through to Roland's house. When he came to the phone I quickly said, "Hey Roland, today's the day, bring your money," and hung up.

We got a ride to Tet Jaune Cache, a small village a couple of hours southeast of Prince George. Roland had called ahead to a couple of girls that he knew there who were going to join us as well. From there we walked together along the railway tracks beside the highway for about an hour and then came up to a line cabin—a sort of rolling bunkhouse used by the crews that work on the tracks. No one was around and it was already evening, so we decided to climb in and spend the night there.

By then Roland and the girls had been reported missing. Someone must have seen us walking along the tracks, because the police knew exactly where to find us. We had just settled in when a policeman's voice called out through a megaphone, telling us to come out. I yelled back that I had a knife, and I was going to hurt someone who was with me if they didn't back off. For the next hour-and-a-half we negotiated back and forth. The police kept talking to us and asking us to give ourselves up and come out, and I kept threatening to hurt someone. I wouldn't have ever hurt any of my friends, but the police didn't know that, and I knew it would buy me some time. While all this was going on, Roland and the girls decided this was a bit too much for them and they really weren't that interested in running away with me after all.

It was a dark, rainy night and there was thick forest right next to the tracks, so when it became clear to me that I was on my own and the standoff with the police wasn't going anywhere I picked up my backpack, jumped out the back window and scrambled into the trees. I heard the police yelling at me, so I ran through the bush for a while. When I felt I had put enough distance between me and them I cut back towards the highway. I saw a dark spot at the bottom of an embankment beside the highway, and as I got closer I could make out that it was a culvert. There was a car coming around the corner about half a mile away, and I was afraid it might be the police, so I quickly ducked inside the culvert before anyone could see me. The culvert was about five feet high, and there was a foot of water rushing through it. It was late spring, and the melt water coming down from the mountains was ice cold. I tried to spread my legs far enough apart to straddle the water, but it was really awkward standing there, hunched over like that. I was using one of those old aluminum frame backpacks, and after a while I discovered that if I laid it across the culvert with the water running beneath it I could lean against it to be a bit more comfortable, though it was still miserable and cold.

It was eerily dark and quiet inside the culvert. The only sounds I could hear were the water rushing below me and the noise of the rain falling on the leaves. I was shivering cold, and it felt like my feet were freezing. I was wearing an old pair of canvas running shoes and a pair of thin socks with no toes or heels on them. I kept trying to lift my feet out of the ice-cold water. They were killing me. While I was standing there I promised myself that if I ever made it in this world I would wear two pairs of good socks every day.

After I had listened to several vehicles drive past I noticed that it was easy to tell which ones were the semis because they made a lot more noise. I could already hear them when they came around the corner a half mile away. I decided I would try to get a ride with one of them, but I didn't dare leave my hiding place because the police were also driving up and down the highway, shining their spotlights into the bush and calling out for me to give myself up. After a couple of hours the traffic started to really slow down, so whenever I heard a semi coming I would step out of the culvert and look up and down the highway. If no other vehicles were around I would scramble up the bank to the shoulder of the road and stick out my thumb. It was a long, cold, miserable night. At around 1:30 a.m. I finally got a ride with a trucker heading into Kamloops.

Traveling was slow after that. I was having trouble getting rides and still watching out for the police. After a couple more days on the road I was getting really hungry. I finally got so desperate for something to eat that I went up to a farmhouse and knocked on the door. When the lady answered I asked her if I could trade my transistor radio for a can of beans or something. She just stood there staring at me. I must have looked quite pitiful and hungry, because she invited me in and used a whole loaf of bread to make me peanut butter and jelly sandwiches. She handed me the sandwiches, and also gave me a couple tins of beans. She told me to keep my radio, and take care of myself. She was a very nice person.

Whenever I was hitchhiking somewhere I would bring a piece of plastic with me to build a shelter for the nights. I would usually try to find a picnic table that I could drape the plastic over. I'd put rocks on the corners to hold it down and then crawl underneath and roll out my sleeping bag. If it was a cold night I'd sometimes light a little fire. So, on this trip that's how I was spending my nights. When I wasn't near a rest stop and there were no picnic tables around I just found a sheltered spot off the road somewhere and wrapped the sheet of plastic around my sleeping bag for the night.

I finally made it into Vancouver, and after looking around for a while I broke into a motel room. I had watched a guy who looked like a construction worker or something drive away. I assumed he wouldn't be back until that evening, so I went in and made myself at home. There was some loose change on top of the dresser, so I stuck it in my pocket and went across the street to a little corner store. I met a couple of girls outside the store, and after we talked for a while we went in, bought a bag of cookies with the change I had found, and stole a bunch of other stuff. Then we went back across the street to the motel room.

The store owner knew we were stealing from him, so he just watched where we went and then called the police. A little later, while I was in the shower, I heard someone knocking on the door. I walked over and opened the door just a crack to look out. When I saw a police uniform I slammed the door shut, chained it and sprinted as fast as I could for the back exit. I grabbed my pants off the bed and flew out the door, still butt naked and dripping wet, and ran full speed right into the outstretched arm of biggest policeman I had ever seen. "Hold on there, son," he said, with a smirk on his face.

I spent the next four hours in the police station answering their questions, but trying to give them as little information as possible. It didn't take them long to get the police reports from Prince George and to find out I was a runaway and that I had, among other things, been threatening people with a knife. I got the feeling they didn't really know what to do with me.

From the police station they brought me straight to the Iris Château, a group home for young violent offenders like me. From the outside it was a big, beautiful house, but on the inside it was nothing short of a prison. I spent the next month there with anywhere from 12 to 18 other kids. Different kids were coming and going all the time. Some just stayed for a few days, and some, like me, stayed for a bit longer.

At night I was locked into a plain 8' x 10' room with nothing in it but a cot and some bedding. There were no other furnishings or fixtures in the room, and the ceiling was so high that it couldn't be reached. I was first sent to the bathroom to clean myself up, and then told to strip down to my underwear. The door was locked until 7:00 a.m. There was a window in the room, but it was far enough behind some bars that I couldn't reach it. When the sun went down it was pitch black. I hated the darkness.

After breakfast each morning we were all sent to work on the line. The Iris Château, besides being a juvenile detention home, was a chicken slaughter house. My job on the line the first morning was to take the chickens out of their crates, hang them up by their feet and cut their heads off. It was where all the new kids started out. They called it "breaking you," because it was a cruel, messy job, and at some point in the day you would break down and start to cry. I was the youngest and smallest kid there, and while we were walking out to the line one of the older guys laughed at me and said, "We're going to break you today." I just ignored him. I knew that no matter how bad it got, no one was going to break me. They had no idea what I had been through.

When I picked up the first chicken it slapped me in the face with its wings and started pecking and scratching at me. I felt bad for killing it because I knew that, like me, it was just trying to survive. Every chicken I picked up flapped and scratched and pecked. They were hurting me, but after I had done a few more I started hurting them back. Hour after hour I stood there getting slapped and scratched and covered with blood, and hour after hour I got angrier and angrier until I had worked myself into an all-out killing spree.

The next morning after breakfast I was ready to get back at it, and I noticed that I had earned a certain measure of respect from the other kids. Or maybe it was fear. I didn't talk, I didn't break and I didn't show any emotion. I just kept on killing. Usually after a few days you got moved up the line to a different position, but I was left right there for my entire stay. After a while I started to get pretty good with a knife, and I began to experiment and to get more creative in how I was cutting and slashing.

I stayed at the Iris Château for a month, and then one day a social worker from Prince George came to pick me up. She seemed like a nice person, and on the drive back home she tried to get me to talk, but I said almost nothing during the whole eight-hour trip. She knew Doris, so she knew that the situation she was bringing me back to was bad, but she had no idea how bad it really was. No one knew how bad it was. If they would have known, I have to believe they surely would have helped me. No decent human being would knowingly leave a child in that kind of environment. Before she dropped me off she told me to be smart and to try staying out of trouble. I was becoming smarter all the time, but asking me to stay out of trouble was asking for the impossible.

I was supposed to be going to school but I didn't bother going back for the rest of the year. I still got on the bus every morning, but I just rode it into town and got off at the pool hall. The driver was a really nice lady. For the morning ride into town I would sit in the seat right behind her, and she would always have some nice things to say to me. Sometimes she would bring me some candies or a chocolate bar. She knew I wasn't going to school, but she never said anything to Doris, and neither did any of my teachers. They all knew it was better if I just stayed away. For her part, Doris either didn't know or didn't care. After school I would go to the bus barns and catch the bus for the ride back home.

Halfway between the school and my bus stop junction there was a small store and a gas station. On the way home the bus would stop there for a couple of minutes, and I started to use this as an opportunity to generate a little income. I would take orders from the other kids on the bus, they would give me 10 or 15 cents, or a quarter if they wanted a bottle of pop, and I would run into the store and pick up whatever they had asked for. I usually paid for about half of the stuff, and the rest of it would find its way up my sleeves, inside my jacket or down my pant leg. The leftover change was mine to keep. I was pretty smooth. I could look the store owner in the eye and talk to him while I was sliding something up my sleeve. He might have suspected I was stealing, but he never caught me.

The pool hall opened at 10:00 a.m., but I would get there around 9:30, and the owner would let me in. I'd wipe down the tables for him, play a song or two from the jukebox with the change I'd earned from the bus run the day before, and have time for a couple games of pool before the other customers started arriving. I was always slamming quarters into the jukebox. The songs told stories of places where I could escape.

The pool hall was a rough place. Prince George is a logging town, and most of the regulars were big, hardened lumberjacks. I watched them hustling, and started to learn a few tricks. After a while I got quite good at stacking a deck of cards for poker pool.

At the pool hall one day I met a guy who introduced himself as Tank. He was a few years older than me, and he said that he was supposed to be in grade 12. I could see right away why people called him Tank. He was 6'-4", and close to 300 lbs. Tank and I hit it off right away and became good friends. He got me started into more serious drugs, and also introduced me to the Red Rock Roller Dome.

The Red Rock Roller Dome was a roller derby track 25 miles from the city in the middle of nowhere. From a distance it looked like a giant igloo. This was the early '70s when roller derby was in its heyday. It's a brutally violent game, where you try to lap your opponents on roller skates around an oval track by any means possible. Fists, elbows, knees and just about anything else goes. The first time I saw it I remember thinking I was born for this. I loved playing the game. It was orchestrated violence, and the more violent it got, the better it was! The score didn't matter to me; it was all about inflicting pain.

On the weekends they would bring in live bands. Two or three hundred people would show up, and there would be muscle cars all over the parking lot. Usually there were just as many people outside as inside. Booze and drugs were everywhere. Brawls would break out and guys would be swinging clubs and chains and sometimes even trying to run each other down with their cars. The police would show up, but they wouldn't dare move in until they were there in numbers. It was pure mayhem, and I loved every bit of it!

About a month after getting back from my stay at the Iris Château I got shot at for the first time in my life. It didn't happen at the Red Rock or the pool hall or any of the other places where I might have expected it. There was an old couple who lived about a half a mile down the road from us. I had cut their lawn the previous summer and shoveled snow for them a few times in the winter. That summer when school was out their granddaughter came to stay with them. She was a couple of years older than me and I thought she was absolutely gorgeous, so I managed to find my way over to their place and introduce myself to her. I was there several times over the next few days. We hit it off quite well and she was starting to flirt with me quite a bit.

One day she called me up to tell me she was going to be alone for the day, so I should come on over and have some fun. I knew exactly what she meant by that. But her grandparents came home earlier than expected that evening and caught us in her bedroom. Grandpa took one look at what was going on, and, in a rather matter-of-fact voice, told me that he was going to kill me. I grabbed my jeans and shoes and headed out the back door as fast as I could run. Something about the look on his face and the sound of those bullets being shoved into the chamber of his gun made me think that he wasn't fooling around. The bush was about 100 feet from their house, and I ducked into the trees just as the first shot whistled past my head. I got the distinct impression that he wasn't just trying to scare me; he was trying to kill me.

A couple of friends of mine, brothers named Richard and Michael, lived about four miles away, and I decided to head for their place. While I was jogging through the bush I could see Grandpa driving up and down the road with his window open and his rifle still in his hand. I made sure I was out of sight every time he came by.

For the next month I stayed with Richard and Michael. I figured that if I went back home the old man would know where to find me, and although getting hurt wouldn't have bothered me too much, the thought of getting killed didn't sit too well with me.

Richard and Michael's mom and dad were honest, good-hearted people. They knew I was a piece of work, but they let me stay in their home where they made me feel welcome. Their dad worked for the Department of Highways—he was one of the smartest people I have ever met. When we were sitting around in the evening we sometimes pulled out the dictionary and tried to stump him with a word. I don't think we ever found a word that he didn't know the meaning of. Along with the definition he could usually also give us the proper spelling, and often even the Latin or Greek origin.

He knew that I wouldn't or couldn't go back home, and he also knew that my dad was coming to get me in a few more weeks. So, whenever I got a bit too wild or did something really stupid he would just patiently tell me to cool it.

Their house was at the end of a long dirt driveway. There were a few times when we snuck out at night after their parents were asleep and took their big black Pontiac Parisienne into Prince George. None of us had a driver's license, but little details like that really didn't concern us a whole lot.

One night we drove down to a strip mall where some older guys in a hot car were having fun and horsing around. We swerved in front of them and gestured a few graphic insults in their direction. They chased us around the city for over an hour before we finally lost them. We'd stop and let them get out of their car and walk right up to us, and then we'd speed off again. The braver and cockier we got, the angrier they got. I don't know what would have happened if they ever would have caught us, but I'm sure it wouldn't have been pretty.

Usually before we brought the car home we made sure the gas tank was filled to the same level as when we took the car, but that night we ended up using a bit more gas than we had planned. We also banged up the car a little bit by hitting a few curbs, so we knew we were busted anyway. It started to rain pretty hard as we were leaving the city, so by the time we got back home their long dirt driveway was nothing but mud. So, we just left the car on the road and walked to the house. Their parents must have been upset, but we never heard anything about it.

There was a group of seven of us who hung around together that summer after school was out. Besides me, Richard and Michael, there was a friend of theirs named Gary, Tank, a guy we called Fish, and my friend from school, Bobby. Bobby was a good kid, but he liked to have fun too, and for us, "fun" usually meant getting into some sort of trouble. That month we had a lot of fun and had a lot of laughs, but it also turned out to be a terribly tragic month.

Bobby had a driver's license. One day he was driving a bunch of us into Prince George when a police car passed us going the other way. We were drinking beer and acting like idiots, and the cop took one look at what was going on, turned around and came after us. Bobby hit the gas and as soon as we topped a hill and were out of sight, we started tossing the beer out the windows. While this was going on, we noticed Gary coming down the highway towards us on his motorbike. We waved, and when he saw us he goosed it, popped his front wheel in the air, and blew past us with a big grin on his face.

That was the last time we saw him alive. While we were doing our best to explain to the police officer that the beer all over the highway wasn't ours he got a call on his radio about a motorcycle accident. Just after Gary had passed us, he had lost control of his bike and was killed.

Later that same week Tank was driving home at 5:00 a.m. after an all-nighter at the Roller Dome. He had a little Datsun B10, and I had often marveled at how such a big guy could cram himself into that little car. That morning he missed the approach to his driveway, slammed into the culvert and was killed on impact. Two weeks later, Fish committed suicide. I had lost three of my friends in a period of three weeks.

The following week Dad and Carol arrived from Ontario to pick me up. I don't even remember if I said goodbye to Doris. I just threw a few things into a small backpack, got into their car and rode away with them.

CHAPTER 5

When Dad and Carol picked me up they were in the middle of their vacation, so instead of going straight back to Wawa, Ont. where they were now living, we toured through Wyoming, North Dakota and South Dakota before heading home. The trip was something different for me, and I kind of enjoyed it. I even managed to stay out of trouble, for the most part. I did hook up with a girl at one of the hotels where we were staying in Wyoming, and things got a little out of hand for a while, but other than that I think I behaved myself quite well.

Carol and I had never gotten along before, and it was no different now. She had become a police officer and was stationed back in Wawa, but to me it seemed she hadn't changed at all. We argued constantly about everything. Dad and I fought, too. Our first night on the road we pulled up to a cabin in Lake Louise. They went inside, and told me to unload the bags from the car. In the process of unloading I somehow managed to get the sleeve of Dad's nice leather coat caught in the trunk latch. Of course, that didn't go over too well, and I learned that his temper was just as volatile as it always had been.

When we got back to Wawa it was the same old story all over again. They lived in a trailer park, and Dad was almost always half-drunk. He wasn't working at the time, so all he did all day was sit around and drink. I was drinking hard, too.

A couple of weeks after we got there I had my first-ever visit to a dentist. I had been having horrible toothaches for years already. Some of my brothers and sisters had gone to a dentist when they were in foster care, but I had never been in the system, so I'd never seen a dentist. There had never been any extra money for that sort of thing, so my teeth were in awful shape. A few months earlier I had been having such terrible toothaches that I wrapped the exposed nerve ending around my finger, pulled it out as far as I could and then sawed it off by scraping it against the jagged edge of a broken tooth. That was some of the most intense pain I have ever felt. If 10.0 on the pain scale is where you pass out, then that was 9.5. The dentist said my teeth were the worst he had ever seen. He pulled out four of them on that first visit.

That fall I started a new school again. It was a small school where all the kids knew each other. I was the new kid, and a cop's kid at that. I again tried to keep to myself and not cause any trouble, but I knew it wouldn't last. I was right about that. Within two months I had made some enemies, and was starting to get into a few scuffles. Nothing too serious had happened, and I was honestly trying to keep it that way. But it all changed one day when I was getting dressed in the locker room after gym class. I was just minding my own business when five older kids came over and started to hassle me. I recognized a couple of them as the older brothers of some kids in my class who I wasn't getting along with. I'm not sure they really wanted to fight; I think they just wanted to rough me up a bit and teach me a lesson, and they probably weren't expecting me to fight back quite so hard. But things went sideways in a hurry.

One of them hit me in the side of the head pretty hard, and that got it going. I was outnumbered, so they eventually beat me up bad enough to put me in the hospital overnight with a concussion, but along the way I got in a few pretty good shots myself. I thought I could look after myself, but after that fight I realized I would need to change a few things if I wanted to make sure nothing like that would ever happen again.

After the fight I was expelled from school for a week. I was told that before I would be allowed back my parents would need to come with me to visit the principal. I think they were supposed to promise that they would make me behave myself, or something like that. I came back at the end of the week with my dad. The principal invited us into his office, and it was obvious to me from the start that he was on some sort of power trip. He started off by saying that the whole thing had been my fault, and since I was the new kid in school I should be making more of an effort to get along with the other kids. Dad had been drinking again, and after about a minute he had heard all he needed. He called the principal an f__ing goof, and then got up and walked out.

That left just the two of us sitting there. The principal started yelling and swearing at me, telling me I was nothing but a piece of garbage and I was no different than my father. He was getting more and more enraged and kept yelling and insulting me. I just sat there quietly, but on the inside I was starting to boil. "Are you too stupid to talk to me?" he finally yelled.

That was all it took. The switch turned on and I instantly flew across the top of his desk. I hit him so hard and so fast that he didn't have time to react. He fell over backwards on his chair with me on top of him. When we hit the floor I was already feeding him with my fists. I hit him at least 15 times in the face before the secretary came running in. She ran right back out screaming and then came back in a few seconds later with the vice principal. I still had the principal down and was pounding on him. His face was already a bloody mess, but I kept hitting him. I looked up at the vice principal and yelled, "Get out of here or I'll kill you, too!" He just froze there for a couple of seconds and then ran out to get more teachers.

When they came back I was just getting up off of the principal. I walked out of the office without anyone laying a finger on me. They all just cleared out of my way. I went down the hall to my locker, yelling and swearing at the top of my lungs. I was kicking in locker doors and throwing around garbage cans and whatever else I could get my hands on. I was completely out of control. Teachers and students came out of the classrooms to see what was going on. I ripped the lock off my locker and threw it as hard as I could at one of the teachers standing there. Then I grabbed my backpack and headed out the door. That was the end of my formal schooling. I never went back to school anywhere after that.

I had beaten the school principal so badly that the police got involved, but all they did was talk to me—no charges were ever laid. They knew that I was being picked on at school, and they also knew that the principal was a bit of a jerk. In the end they decided it was just a bad situation and I was a violent, out-of-control kid, so nothing ever came of it.

Just before Christmas that year, Carol went away for a three-week training course at the police academy. Before she left, she bought a case of Magnus' White Rum. She tied a ribbon around each bottle and was planning to give one to each of the guys at the police station as a Christmas gift. When she left, she stuck the bottles in her closet. She really should have known better than that.

I had been drinking as much of dad's booze as I could get away with, but he was starting to notice that it was disappearing a lot faster than he was drinking it. I knew I had to back off drinking his booze, and that rum was just sitting there. The first night after Carol was gone I decided I would just help myself to a sip or two. I took a razor blade, carefully cut the seal and removed the cap. I drank half a bottle that night. The next night I finished it off. Over the course of the next three weeks I drank every drop of rum from all twelve bottles. After I emptied each bottle I carefully replaced the cap and ribbon and put it back exactly as it was. When I was done, it looked like they hadn't even been touched. When Carol came home I didn't feel the need to tell her that the rum was gone, so the bottles just sat there.

About a week before Christmas she invited the guys from the station over for a party. I volunteered to go and get the rum because I knew that if she picked up the case I'd be busted. Actually, I knew I would be busted at some point that evening anyway, but I thought I'd buy as much time as possible. I put the case on the coffee table in the living room and Carol told the guys they could each take a bottle on their way home after the party.

About halfway through the evening one of the policemen reached over and picked up his bottle. He hesitated for a moment and then looked over at me. When he saw the smile on my face he started to laugh and told the guy sitting beside him to take his bottle. He picked up a bottle, they looked at each other and said, "Cheers." The other guys all started grabbing their bottles. When they found out the bottles were all empty they just lost it and started laughing. We all just kept drinking. Everyone got smashed that night.

Carol must have been upset, but she never really came down on me for that one. It was clear that she hated me, but there was something about the bad boy side of me that she seemed to admire. Maybe it was some of that same unpredictable, volatile personality that was in my dad, and that she seemed to find attractive.

After Christmas I started spending my days just hanging around the pool hall. That's where I met my friend, Johnboy. He was 15 years old, six months older than me, but he was already living on his own. Until that fall he had been living with his mom in Timmons, Ont., but when school started he decided he didn't really want to go, so he stuck out his thumb and hitchhiked west. He got as far as Wawa where he got a job in a restaurant and found a room to rent in a local boarding house.

His mom worked in a butcher shop in Timmons, and every day after school Johnboy had gone there to hang around for a couple of hours until her shift was done. He passed the time by playing with knives, and after a while he got pretty good. He could pick up a knife in each hand and spin them around so fast that it would mesmerize everyone in the room. It was amazing what he could with a knife.

Over the next couple of years his knife work would get us out of quite a few tricky situations. He really wasn't any good at fighting, but he would get those knives spinning, and while everyone was looking at him I'd go clock someone in the side of the head. That little element of surprise would either give us the early upper hand or give us enough time to clear out.

For that winter though, it was just small-time stuff. He was a good pool player, better than me at the time, and I had already learned a fair bit about hustling. So we teamed up and passed that winter at the pool hall. We challenged anyone at any game. If it involved a ball and a stick, we played it. If we didn't know the game being played, we learned it. We were quite young, and there were better players than us, but we were better hustlers. We never played for any serious money— just enough for fries and gravy and maybe a bottle of pop. Sometimes people knew we were scamming them, but they could never quite prove it. We got in a few fights when people didn't want to pay, but that didn't happen very often. We had a lot of fun that winter, and along the way we became a good team.

Partway through that winter I got a part-time job at a grocery store bagging groceries and stocking shelves. The owners knew I was a rough kid, but they were willing to give me a chance. I worked hard and did my jobs well, so they were happy with me and treated me well.

Johnboy and I kept hustling at the pool hall between our shifts. One day I brought him home to meet my dad. I had told Dad about this kid who was a pretty good pool player, and that we had been hustling together. Dad seemed at least mildly interested because he was a hustler too, so I thought he might like to meet him. It was the middle of the afternoon and Dad was already more than a little drunk. He was standing at the kitchen counter having a cigarette, and when I introduced Johnboy he looked at him and said, "I hear you can play pool, but can you fight?" Then he put on some oven mitts and started taking shots at his head.

I stepped in and said, "Leave him alone, he didn't do anything! We're not trying to start nothin' here."

Dad looked at me and said, "So, you think you're big enough to take on the old man now?" He took a swing at me and I ducked out of the way. I was nearly eyeball to eyeball with him, and we stood there glaring at each other for a couple of seconds. I had been waiting for this for a long time. This wasn't just about Johnboy. It was about Scottie, and Rena, and all the times he had slapped me around. It was about all those years of drinking and sexual abuse.

I took a swing at him and we fought from the kitchen all the way down the trailer through the living room and into the hallway by the bedrooms. I was going backwards because he was hitting me harder than I was hitting him, but I was mad and was getting in a few pretty good shots myself. At some point I made the mistake of hitting him hard enough to get him angry. He kicked me in the groin and then gave me an upper cut that put the lights out. At least I think it was an upper cut. I woke up a while later out in the middle of the front yard with an aching jaw.

The first thought that went through my mind was, "That was worth it." Dad had gotten the better of me, but I knew that I had gotten in a few shots. More than that, I'd stuck up for myself and for my friend. It felt good. I picked myself up, wiped off the dust and blood, and Johnboy and I went over to his place. That was the last I had to do with my dad. I moved in with Johnboy.

Early that summer I quit my job at the grocery store and went to work at a gas station just down the highway. All summer, big motorhomes were rolling along the highway and stopping there to fill up with gas, and I knew I could make more money hustling the tourists than I could bagging groceries. The place was a tourist trap that sold all sorts of souvenirs. One of the most popular souvenirs was amethyst—a violet-colored quartz found in nearby quarries. Some of the bigger pieces would go for as much as $200. I found I could do a pretty good business selling it at a discounted price right at the pump. As long as I wasn't too greedy the managers never noticed pieces were going missing. After a while, I was making a lot more money selling amethyst than I was from my wages.

Chapter 6

Johnboy and I figured the world wasn't that complicated, and we could probably just make our way by hustling and playing pool. We were getting restless just sitting around Wawa though, so we decided we would work through the summer and then head for B.C. With his tips and what I was making from my little side business selling amethyst we figured we could save up enough money to buy a motorbike and ride out west. A couple of weeks later we had scraped together the cash to buy a used Kawasaki 250 triple stroke. It was a fast little bike. Neither of us had ever driven a motorbike before, but the guy we bought it from gave us a quick lesson, and we drove it away.

We didn't bother to put plates on it, and neither of us had a license. I couldn't have gotten a license even if I had wanted one because I had just turned 15. But that didn't matter. We rode that bike everywhere. We loved the feeling of freedom it gave us.

We had owned the bike for about three weeks when I was riding home from work one day and noticed that the police were following me. They knew we had been riding all over town without a license, and they had been looking for a chance to catch us in the act. I wasn't about to give them that chance, so I hit the throttle and took off down the road. I wasn't afraid of them or too worried about what they would do to me. The truth was, most of the guys on the force liked me. They knew I had a personality, and I think they were just hoping I would grow up and move out of town, and not end up like my dad. The only cop who didn't like me was Carol.

The gas station where I worked was on the outskirts of town. I was going a bit faster than I should have been as I came down the highway and around a corner into the residential area. I looked up and saw a couple of little kids playing out on the street. I knew right away that if I tried to take the corner there was no way I could avoid them, so I hit the back brake, popped the front end up in the air and crashed into a guard rail going about 60 kilometres an hour. The bike was destroyed and I went flying over the handlebars and down an embankment.

I landed flat on a rock and the bone in my leg snapped in two, just above my knee. As soon as I hit the ground I knew my leg was broken. I looked down and saw that the bone was actually sticking right out through my jeans. The police helped me up the embankment and then put me in the back seat of the cruiser and drove me to the hospital.

They walked me to the front desk where the nurse was looking down, doing some paperwork. I limped up to her and said, "Excuse me, I think my leg is broken." She never bothered to look up from her work. She just said, somewhat condescendingly, "Young man, if you had a broken leg you wouldn't be standing there right now, would you?"

I hobbled a few steps back so she could see the bone sticking out and said, "I don't know, it looks broken to me."

I wouldn't do it again just to see the look on her face, but it was priceless.

I had learned by this time to withstand incredible amounts of pain. I had taught myself to actually ride the rush. I would anticipate the pain and just ride it until I crossed the line where my body would go into shock and I would pass out. Just before you pass out you start to feel warm all over, like warm water running over you. I had been there so often that I had learned to wait for that feeling. It didn't matter how much pain I had to endure. Pain didn't matter anymore.

After lying in my hospital room for three days, who should walk in but Carol the cop! She slapped some papers down on my cast sending waves of pain up my leg and through my entire body. "We got you now, you little S.O.B." she said. She then went on to tell me that I was being charged with resisting arrest, dangerous driving, having no license or insurance, and a whole list of other offenses—basically whatever they could think of. She told me that I wouldn't be anybody's problem again until I turned 18, because this time I would definitely be going off to juvie. She went on a little rant for the next few minutes, using some fairly graphic profanity to let me know I wasn't exactly the most wonderful thing that had ever happened in her world. She compared me to my dad, so I found out that day what she really thought of him—not much, as it turned out. She never did ask how I was doing or if I needed anything. When she was done, she just grinned and said, "See you in court." Then she turned and walked out.

As I lay there thinking about what she had said, I realized I might have actually gotten myself into some serious trouble this time. Being sent to juvie for the next few years didn't appeal to me at all, so I told Johnboy we needed to step up our plan for going to B.C. We talked about it and decided I should try to stay in the hospital as long as I could to get healed up, and he would get everything ready so we could hit the road just before my court date, which was coming up in about three weeks.

For the next three weeks the nurses tried to get me up and walking, but I whined and cried and made it seem like I was in way too much pain to move. I didn't want them thinking I was well enough to be sent home. Johnboy came by every day to visit, and we kept fine-tuning our plan for heading out west. I had learned by now that food isn't always easy to come by when you're out on the road, so I saved all those little peanut butter and jam packages that came with my meals, and Johnboy took them home after his visits.

I was in the hospital for a total of 23 days before we decided it was time to make a break for it. I had been timing the nurses and noticed that they made their rounds every half hour during the day, at quarter to and quarter after the hour, but after midnight they only came around once an hour. That evening when Johnboy left he went out the fire exit and put a piece of duct tape across the latch so it wouldn't lock. I stayed in bed watching the nurses make their rounds, and pretended to be asleep. At 1:45 a.m. the nurse stuck her head in my door and saw that everything was quiet, just like it had been an hour before. As soon as she was gone, I swung my cast over the side of the bed and hobbled down to the end of the hall where Johnboy was waiting at the fire exit. He had our backpacks stuffed with our few clothes and belongings and three weeks' worth of peanut butter and jam.

We headed straight for the edge of town and sat down under the Big Goose. Anyone who has been to Wawa has seen the goose. It's one of the most recognizable landmarks along the Trans Canada Highway. There, behind the giant goose, Johnboy took out a pair of tin snips and cut the cast off my leg. My leg was really sore, but if we were going to make any kind of decent time we knew we had to get the cast off. A few of the stitches got ripped open in the process, and my leg started to bleed. It smelled awful, and when I looked at it I knew it was going to give me trouble. I had been injured often enough to know what would heal and what was going to be a problem, and I could see right away that my leg wasn't good. I didn't say anything to Johnboy though, because we had to get going.

We started hitchhiking and got a few rides so that a day-and-a-half later we were just outside of the Lake of the Woods area in northwestern Ontario. My leg was badly swollen, and I was starting to feel like I was going to black out, so we decided to rest there in the ditch beside the highway for a while. We could see a stream just down the embankment, so Johnboy went to get some water. While he was gone I laid down, leaned against my pack and passed out.

I don't remember what happened next because I was out cold, but Johnboy told me later that as he was on his way to get the water, a motorhome pulled over to let some traffic go past. The lady in the passenger seat looked over and saw me lying there. He scrambled back up the bank as fast as he could, but by the time he got to the top they were already standing over me. He yelled and told them to leave me alone, but she explained that she was a nurse and said that she just wanted to help. Johnboy knew that I was in bad shape, so he let them bring me inside their motorhome.

They were on their way to the States for a vacation, but when they realized what kind of shape I was in, they parked there in a campground. For the next two days I slipped in and out of consciousness. They wanted to take me to a hospital, but Johnboy begged them not to do that. They were really nice to us, and stayed there with us for three days altogether so that she could look after me. She cleaned my leg, fed us, did our laundry and sewed up my jeans.

They were curious about what we were doing, so we told them as much of our story as we thought we could. After three days I was feeling a lot better, so they asked if we wanted to continue on, or if they could take us to the police station where we could get some help. We told them that we wanted to just be on our way, so she hugged us and wished us well. As they drove away we looked at each other and agreed that they were some really nice people.

After they had driven off, we started taking stock of what we had with us, and talking about how lucky we were. I reached into my pocket and felt something there. I pulled it out and I saw that it was a $1 bill. Then I reached into my other pocket and found some more bills. We started searching and found that they had stuffed $50 in small bills into my clothes. We were blown away. Neither of us had ever experienced that kind of unconditional love, and we weren't really sure how to feel about it. It felt good, but it also felt strange. We were used to scamming people out of their cash, but here was a couple who had already been so kind to us now giving us money out of the goodness of their hearts. It was something completely foreign to us. I just stood there and thought, "Wow! That's really amazing."

Looking back now, I can see that this was one of the many times when God directly intervened in my life. I could have easily died right there beside the highway, but He sent the right person along at exactly the right time. Back then I didn't see it, but I know now that God was watching over me.

They had taken us as far as the west side of Winnipeg before dropping us off, so again we started walking and hitchhiking from there. We didn't get any rides that evening, so we pitched our tent on the grass in the middle of the divided highway and settled in for the night. Early in the morning we heard a car go racing by, come screeching to a stop, and then squeal its tires backing up. My first thought was that we were in trouble, and maybe a gang or someone was going to beat us up. That's just the first place my mind naturally went.

We got out of the tent just as this guy jumped out of a big four-door sedan. We could see right away that he was flying higher than a kite. He was strung right out and started asking questions a mile a minute. "How you guys doin'? Are you heading west? Do you want a ride?"

We looked at each other and said, "Sure."

"Great!" he said. "I'll go back and get some gas and some munchies and I'll pick you up in 10 minutes." Then he jumped back into his car, squealed his tires and took off at the same breakneck speed.

We were packed up and waiting at the side of the highway in five minutes. We sat there waiting for what seemed like quite a while, and just when we decided we had been screwed and he wasn't coming back, he came flying towards us and screeched to a stop. We were beginning to realize that everything this guy did was at top speed. We weren't quite sure what to think of him just yet, so while he was away Johnboy and I had decided he would sit in the front seat beside this guy and I would sit in the back with my knife ready, in case he tried anything and I needed to take control of the situation. That became the arrangement on most of our rides. Johnboy was a smooth talker who could carry on a conversation with anyone, and I was the one who could step in if things ever turned ugly.

It didn't take long for us to relax, especially when he started offering us his drugs. He was taking speed, something neither of us had ever tried. But we started taking it, and all three of us were flying high all the way to B.C. It was a crazy couple of days. He drove like a madman the whole way. People couldn't get out of his way fast enough. He was passing trucks on the shoulder of the road. Sometimes Johnboy would steer while he just kept his foot to the floor and did more drugs. The fact that we got there in one piece was nothing short of a miracle.

We spent one night in Calgary, and the next evening pulled into a little town somewhere in the mountains of southeastern B.C., where we got a motel room for the night. After tossing our stuff into the room we went into town and picked up a few groceries. We also hooked up with a couple of girls who came back to the room with us. One of the things we bought at the store was a bag of pomegranates. None of us had ever had a pomegranate before, but they looked good. They tasted alright, but we found it was a lot more fun just throwing them around the room. They left a nice red stain wherever they hit the wall.

Our friend with the car was the only one who was registered, so the motel owner wasn't overly impressed when he knocked on the door later that night to tell us to cool it and found five of us partying and pretty much tearing the room apart. We were doing drugs and it was getting pretty wild. When he saw what was going on, he told us he was going to call the police. We told him it would be better for all of us, him included, if he didn't do that. We said that if he would just give us a few minutes to pack up, we would be on our way. He looked us over and told us we had 10 minutes to get out. We threw our stuff into the car, said goodbye to the girls  and hit the road again. It was five minutes, tops, and we were gone. We didn't want to take a chance on the police showing up.

The next day Johnboy and I traveled with our friend as far as Cranbrook. From there he was heading for Vancouver, but Johnboy and I wanted to go to Prince George. I still had family there, and I wanted to see Rena again. Rena and I had always been close, and I missed her. She had always been the apple of my eye, and I really wanted to see her again.

The next ride we got was from a middle-aged guy with a crew cut. He was a fast talker and a self-professed hustler. He told us he had been hustling his whole life and was making good money at it. He said that if we would stick with him he could teach us everything we needed to know. Johnboy wanted to go with him, but I didn't like him at all. I had spent enough time around scammers and users, and this guy was giving me a bad feeling. He took us as far as Williams Lake, and that evening while we were eating supper in a restaurant Johnboy and I had a pretty heated argument about whether or not we should stick with him. We started yelling at each other and making such a disturbance that the police were called.

They were going to take us down to the station and throw us into a cell for the night, but when they saw that we were just a couple of kids they dropped us off at a hostel instead. This was the 1970s, and people were hitchhiking all over the place, so we just fit in with everyone else.

The next morning we were still mad at each other, and for a while it looked like we might even split up. I made it clear that there was no way I was going with this guy, because I didn't trust him. Finally Johnboy agreed and we again hit the road together.

We got a ride that morning back down the highway to Cache Creek. When we got into town we went to the bus stop where we could get a cheap bowl of soup. While we were having our lunch a couple of girls about our age got off a bus, and we could tell right away that they were runaways like us. We started talking to them, and found out they were from Prince George and were on their way to Vancouver. We were still thinking of heading to Prince George, but after we talked to them for a while we decided the four of us would just head out east together and see what happened. They cashed in the remainder of their bus tickets, and we went out to the highway and started hitchhiking. That afternoon we got a ride into Kamloops from a guy in a pickup truck. He seemed a little suspicious about four kids traveling together, but he gave us a ride anyway. Again Johnboy sat in the front with him while the girls and I jumped into the back.

At Kamloops we thanked him for the ride and then went down to the river to set up our tent. The girls were new to the whole concept of running away, and they had brought way too much stuff with them, so that evening we threw about half of their clothes and things into the river. That wasn't the wisest thing we had ever done, because the girls had been reported missing, and when their clothes were found floating down the river the worst was naturally assumed. When the guy who had given us a ride in his pickup truck heard the news and the description of the missing girls, he called the police and filled in a few more details. He must have told them a pretty good story because the next day we turned on our radio and heard that the police were asking for assistance in locating two young men fitting our description who were possibly armed and dangerous. That's when the girls decided they wanted to go home. That was enough adventure for them.

We travelled with them and made sure they got back home safely to Prince George and then decided to stay there ourselves. That had been our intent all along, anyway.

We rented a room at the Sportsman Inn for $23 a week. It was just two blocks from the pool hall, so we agreed that's where we would set up shop. We spent the next year there, playing pool, hustling, fighting and learning how to survive.

CHAPTER 7

Johnboy and I weren't old enough to be renting a motel room, but by the end of the week we always had the cash in hand, and that seemed to be good enough for the lady who owned the place. That year we lived like kings. We slept in as long as we wanted and got up whenever we felt like it. We played pool, hustled, sold pot and partied. We were too young to get into the liquor store for our booze, so we'd hustle some older guy in a game of pool, and then offer to give him half his money back if he'd get us a bottle of rye. Usually that worked quite well.

It was a rough area of town where a lot of lumberjacks hung out, so we witnessed some pretty good fights, and got involved in a few ourselves. Most days we were in the pool hall by around 11:00 a.m. We'd start shooting a few balls around and practicing some shots, and it wouldn't be long before a few other customers would start trickling in. We'd size them up and then challenge them to whatever game they wanted to play. It didn't matter to us—snooker, 8-ball, 9-ball, pea pool, 101—we played them all, and what we lacked in pool skills we made up for in hustling. We may not have been great pool players, but we were great hustlers. Whatever game was being played, there was always an angle to hustle someone out of their money.

Our favourite game was poker pool. Everyone is dealt five cards and the first one to shoot down all the matching balls is the winner. All the other players have to pay out for each ball they have left on the table. Of course, you keep your cards hidden from the other players, but by now I had developed quite a gift for stacking the deck, so I always knew which balls everyone was shooting at. If I couldn't get a clean shot at any of my balls I'd make sure that Johnboy was set up for his shots, and that the other guys were blocked. I would also make sure that Johnboy and I had a few of the same cards in our hands. That way we would be working on the same balls. It was supposed to be cut-throat (every player for himself), so when Johnboy would win, like he usually did, I would swear at him, call him a lucky S.O.B. and throw my money down on the table. It wouldn't look good if I was dealing and winning, so I had to make it look like I was losing just as much money as everyone else. Then, before anyone else could pick up the cards, I'd scoop them up and deal again. We'd let the other guys win just enough so they'd think it was an honest game. Sometimes they figured out they were getting scammed, and there were also a few times we had to fight for our money, but we ended up doing quite well for ourselves.

The pool hall was owned by a Greek couple who liked us, and took us under their wing. They knew we were out on our own, so they looked out for us. Nick ran the place in the evenings, and his wife Vhasa was there during the day.

The pool hall was located on the second floor of a beautiful new building on the corner of the block. The old building had burned down a couple of years earlier under somewhat mysterious circumstances. Nothing was ever proven though, so the insurance money paid for the new building. Besides running the pool hall, Nick also dabbled in real estate, and owned a couple of other businesses. We learned that he was well connected to people who could pull the right strings and make things happen.

Vhasa was a class act all the way. She was a tall, elegant woman in her mid-40s who did everything in a refined and dignified way. I thought of her as a queen, and if she was then we were her favourite subjects. She liked us from the first day we walked into the place. She told us we were beautiful kids, but ignorant. She taught us our manners and showed us how to treat a lady. She told us to sit properly at the table, to be more respectful and, when she thought we were swearing too much, to expand our vocabulary. I absolutely adored her.

On the few occasions when we lost a game of pool and couldn't pay Vhasa would just go over to the cash register and give us the money to cover it. She treated us well. When the weather turned cold that winter, she called me over one day and slipped a brand new sweater over my head. She told me she had bought it for herself but it didn't fit, so she had no use for it. It fit me perfectly, so she said I should keep it. Later that night when I took it off and looked at the tag I saw that it was a men's size small. I knew she would never have bought a men's sweater for herself. She had gone out and bought it just for me.

After a while she also started bringing sandwiches for us to the pool hall. She knew we weren't really looking after ourselves, so she tried to make sure we were at least eating properly. When we got into fights she would ask if we were okay, and then tell us to clean ourselves up in the washroom. She was patient with us, but also firm. When we played a song on the jukebox she didn't like (such as the Pink Floyd song, "We Don't Need No Education"), she told us to not play it anymore. "That's a bad song," she said. "Education is good. You need education." We didn't agree. We thought life was just fine the way we were living it.

I was getting to know a few of the regulars at the pool hall quite well, so one night after closing they invited me to a guy's house for a few drinks. There were eight or nine guys there, all several years older than me, and they were taking shots of Everclear, the hardest liquor you can get—190 proof, or 95% alcohol. Usually it's mixed with other drinks, but they were drinking it straight. One of them handed me a glass and asked if I was man enough to join them. I put it to my mouth and tipped it back. It came straight back up just as fast as it had gone down. My eyes were watering, and they were all laughing so hard I thought they'd wet themselves. I heard someone ask, "Have you had enough, or are you going to party with the boys?"

As soon as I caught my breath I smiled and said, "In for a penny, in for a pound." I wasn't sure what that meant, but I had heard someone say it at the pool hall, and it seemed to fit.

"In for a pound?" One of them said, "Bring out the coke!" Someone went to the next room and came back with a small bag of white powder. They made some lines on the coffee table and started snorting the cocaine through a straw. I had never tried the stuff before, but I watched them, and when it was my turn I put the straw to my nose and inhaled with all the flair I could muster.

I was instantly in the softest, most comfortable place I had ever been. The world felt so good, so fast. I felt like I was literally floating in a cloud. I sat back and waited for my next turn. I had found a new love. For the next few years, though I didn't go looking for cocaine, I was always up for it whenever it was offered. What I didn't know was that by the time I turned

19 I would be a hardcore addict, and the thing I loved would also be the thing I hated. It would become my consuming passion and my personal hell.

One night, Johnboy and I hustled a couple of guys in their early 20s who thought they were some kind of hotshots. They were getting really mad at Johnboy because he was doing most of the winning again. They kept trying to get their money back, and we kept taking more from them. When they finally decided they'd had enough, they owed us $150. They didn't want to pay, but after we gave them the choice between paying up or eating the butt end of a pool cue, they saw things our way and handed over the money. Before they left, they made sure to threaten us and tell us we shouldn't have messed with them. We just laughed.

Later that night, we walked the five or six blocks to Boston Pizza for supper. We had done quite well that evening, so we planned to celebrate over a plate of pasta. Just as we were coming up to the restaurant, a VW Bug came screeching around the corner and skidded to a stop beside us. The passenger window rolled down and a big gun pointed at us— at least it sure looked big from where I was standing, just a few feet away. There were four guys in the car, and I recognized the one holding the gun as one of the guys from the pool hall earlier that evening.

"Give us back our money," he said, "or I'll put a bullet in your head." It didn't look to me like he was fooling around.

I stared at the gun for a couple of seconds and then pointed over at Johnboy. "Why would you shoot me?" I asked, "He's got the money!"

I did have the money—I never let Johnboy carry it. But I needed some time to decide how I was going to handle this, and it was all I could think of at the moment. Johnboy didn't exactly appreciate being used as a decoy. It caught him completely off guard, so he just stood there with his mouth open and a look of total shock on his face.

"Come on, Richard," he said nervously. "Just give him the money."

"I don't have the money," I said. "You've got the money."

This went back and forth for a while, with the guy holding the gun getting angrier all the time, and Johnboy getting more fidgety and nervous. He kept pleading with me to just give them back their money, and I went right on insisting that I didn't have it. The guy with the gun kept looking back and forth at us, not knowing what to do. Finally he yelled, "I don't care who has the money! I'll shoot you both!"

By then I had the solution figured out (or at least I hoped I did). I took a couple of steps toward the car and pulled a Louis L'Amour book out of my back pocket. I had been reading Louis L'Amour westerns in between games when it was slow at the pool hall. I found them entertaining. I especially liked the way the Sackett boys took care of their problems. I stepped forward to the edge of the curb and started talking to the guy holding the gun. "Hey buddy," I said, "I've been reading these Louis L'Amour books, so let me just sit down here and read this while you shoot me." Then I sat down on the curb and started to take off my boots. My knife was attached to the side of my boot, and I was close enough now to be within striking distance.

The whole thing was getting pretty tense. He was still yelling and threatening to shoot us, his friends in the car were starting to get a little jumpy, and Johnboy was pleading more desperately all the time for me to just hand over the money. I was sitting there taking off my boots and waiting for just the right time to make my move on his gun hand. All I needed was for him to get distracted or look away for a second and I would slash his arm.

Just then somebody came out of the restaurant and started walking down the sidewalk in our direction. He was looking down at something he had in his hand, which I thought was maybe his restaurant receipt, so he hadn't even seen us.

I was still looking for a diversion, so I called out to him, "Hey buddy, come here and see this! This guy's going to shoot us!"

He looked up and said, "Hey, is that a gun? What are you guys doing?" He picked up his pace and kept coming toward us.

The guy with the gun yelled once more, "Come on, give me the f__ing money!" His friends had seen enough. The driver popped the clutch and they took off. We smiled to the guy on the sidewalk, and then walked into the restaurant and ordered our meal.

I thought everything had turned out quite well, and was feeling pretty good about it. No one had gotten shot, and we still had our $150. Johnboy didn't see it quite the same way. I tried to laugh it off and told him he was taking the whole thing way too personally, but he didn't think it was very funny. The rift that had come between us when we had argued in Williams Lake about going with the hustler started to open up again. It would continue to widen over the next few months. That night was the beginning of the end for me and Johnboy.

Another time when we were playing pool with four other guys, this big guy named Garth, who was a pool hall regular, started getting mad and threatening us. He was big and violent enough that he could have snapped us in half if we'd ever let him get his hands on us, but he was also a bit slow because of a brain injury. A few years earlier, he had tried to shoot himself in the head, but because he hadn't been holding the gun at quite the right angle when he pulled the trigger the bullet went up through his chin and then simply lodged into the side of his brain. The doctors decided it was too risky to remove it, so his suicide attempt had left a bullet in his head and a scar under his chin where the barrel of the gun had rested.

He was getting really mad at Johnboy and accusing us of hustling. Of course we were hustling, but we weren't about to admit that to him or anyone else either. I knew that if I could get him to the place where he crossed the line and lost control of his anger we wouldn't have anything to worry about. So I started swearing at him and calling him a big goof. He was getting madder all the time, but I didn't think he was quite mad enough yet. So after a while I stuck my finger up against my chin and said, "Hey, Garth, you're so stupid you can't even pull a trigger properly."

That really got him going. He broke a cue over the table and then spent the next 10 minutes chasing me around the pool hall with it. I was running around tables, ducking under tables and staying just far enough out of his reach to absolutely enrage him. Whenever he seemed to be slowing down, I would stick my finger under my chin and say "Bang!" Then he'd yell, turn red in the face and come at me again. The whole thing was a big comic show, with everyone splitting their guts laughing. After about 10 minutes I led him out the door and then ran back inside and locked the door. He stood there pounding on it for the next five minutes and then walked away. That was all in a day's work for us. That's the way we made our living.

After we'd been living in Prince George for about a year, Johnboy and I decided to take a month off and go back to Wawa. We thought maybe a change of scenery would be nice. My leg had healed up completely by then, so we packed up a few things and hit the road.

When we were hitchhiking we would sometimes play a game we called "Expressions." As a car approached, one of us would call out an expression—afraid, angry, confused, surprised, depressed, or whatever popped into our heads— then we'd have to quickly act it out. Some of the drivers who sped past us must have wondered what we were doing, but it made for some good laughs.

A couple of days after we got back to Wawa, I ran into my brother Ray. He was leaning against the side of a building after he had injected. We talked for a few minutes, and he told me he was living on the streets. He thought it was pretty cool that I was out on my own, too. But I remember walking away thinking that I didn't want to end up like him, and wondered if this was the last time I would ever see my brother alive.

Seeing Ray like that scared me, and got me thinking seriously about what I wanted to do with my life. I knew I could make it on the streets and I could hustle for a living, but I wanted to do something more.

The next afternoon we were walking along the street when we noticed a poster for an army recruiting meeting at the town hall. Johnboy wasn't interested, but I was intrigued, so I decided to go. I thought maybe the army could give me what I was looking for. I knew there was a lot of rage and energy built up inside of me and that if I didn't find some way to either release it or control it, my life was going to get ugly. The army offered discipline, education, food and shelter—just the things I needed. I told myself I had to give it a try.

At the meeting I found out you couldn't get into the army until you were 17 years old, but at 16, like I was, you could still apply and be put through the recruitment process. That sounded alright to me. I signed up, and a couple of days later they loaded all of us recruits onto a bus to Sudbury for three days of written, physical and psychological testing.

I tried my best, and thought I did quite well (except maybe on the temperament part where I must admit I was a bit too quick to lose my cool). I was hopeful that I had made it. But after the three days of testing they told me I wasn't fit for the army because my feet were too bad. I had never worn proper fitting shoes when I was a kid, so my toes were curled under, and I was flatfooted. Because of this, they said I'd never be able to make it on the long marches. They were also quite inquisitive about all my broken bones and the number of scars all over my body.

I begged them to give me a chance, but they said that my feet just weren't good enough for the army. They assured me that my determination and energy weren't an issue—it was my feet. They tried to be nice about it, but I was devastated. On the bus back to Wawa the negative messages I'd heard all my life kept playing over and over in my mind: "You're no good. You'll never amount to anything. You'll never make it. You're good for nothing." I could hear Doris yelling inside my head. "I wish you'd never been born. I should have killed you."

Johnboy and I headed back to Prince George a couple of weeks later. I decided that trying to make something more of myself wasn't worth it, so I'd just go make a living at the pool hall. I started drinking and smoking more, and could feel myself getting angrier on the inside.

One day while I was playing pool, I noticed a bit of an argument taking place a few tables over. I overheard enough to know that a wager had been made, but somebody didn't want to pay up. The guy who wasn't getting paid was getting pretty hot, but he wasn't doing anything about it. After I finished my game, I went over and asked him what was going on.

"That guy over there owes me 1,000 bucks," he said. "I know he's got the money, but he won't pay."

"So why don't you go get it?" I asked.

"Yeah, right!" he said.

It was obvious this guy wasn't a fighter. "I'd give somebody half if they'd collect it for me," he went on.

I'm sure he wasn't expecting me to jump at the opportunity. I was just a scrawny kid, and they were big lumberjacks. He was just complaining about being ripped off.

"Really?" I asked. "You'll give me 500 bucks if I get your money?"

"Sure," he shrugged. I still don't think he expected me to actually do anything about it.

I walked up behind the guy who owed him the money while he was lining up a shot. I waited for the opportune moment, then hit him across the back of the head so hard with my pool cue that I knocked him out cold. I had been knocked out so many times myself that I knew exactly where and how hard to hit him. Finally, all my childhood experiences were paying off. While he was slumped over the table I reached into his pocket and took out his wallet. I counted out $500 for me and $500 for the other guy, and then stuffed his wallet back into his pocket. I could have taken more money, but that wouldn't have been right.

This had been a good payday, but it wasn't only about the money. In my mind it was just as much about sticking up for the underdog. I had always hated it when someone was getting pushed around. Way back in elementary school I had stuck up for George for the same reason. I got mad whenever I saw a bully pushing his weight around. A lot of the school fights I had been in were because I had stepped in when someone was getting picked on. I never fought for any reason other than to defend myself or because I thought it was the right thing to do. But this $500 got me thinking. This was the easiest money I had ever made, and I knew there had to be a lot more where that came from. There were always problems that needed solving, and I knew that I had the ability and the resourcefulness to solve them.

At that point my entrepreneurial spirit kicked in, and "problem-solving," as I liked to call it, became a bit of a sideline for me. At first it was just little jobs—collecting a debt here or there, or making sure that someone got the protection they needed. I was quite happy just leaving it at that. Johnboy and I were still living hand-to-mouth. We were just trying to make enough to pay the hotel bill every week, get one good meal a day at Boston Pizza and hopefully have enough left over at the end of the day to buy some drugs or a bottle of rye. But opportunities kept coming my way, and solving other people's problems started to pay off.

One day I was asked to get rid of a high-end vehicle that someone wanted to collect insurance on. I hot-wired it, took it out of town, lit it on fire and sent it over the cut banks along the Nechako River. That put another quick $1,000 into my pocket.

Nick also started paying me for my services. Whenever he went out of town for a while to look after one of his business interests, he asked me to watch over the place and look out for Vhasa. He also owned a block of rental houses he wanted to tear down to make way for a new supermarket development on the land. The houses were in bad shape and the plumbing and electricity had already been turned off, but the transients and hippies living in them needed to be removed. The police weren't all that interested in getting involved in the situation, and Nick was never too eager to work too closely with them anyway. So, he asked me and Johnboy to take care of it for him.

A couple of nights later we went through the place from one end of the block to the other, kicking in doors, smashing windows, tearing up walls, and completely ransacking every house. In some cases we had to physically remove a few people, but for the most part everyone cleared out ahead of us.

As time went on I kept finding more ways to expand my problem-solving business. There were always drugs to be picked up, delivered somewhere or sold. There were drug debts that needed to be collected. There were scores that needed to be settled. There were a lot of problems, and wherever there was a problem, there was money to be made.

In the years to come the jobs would keep getting bigger and bigger, and so would the money. With more money would come nicer cars, expensive clothes, the best hotels and restaurants, women and, of course, more drugs. I was starting down a road that would take me to places I could never have even dreamed about. For the time though, I was just having fun and living for the rush.

CHAPTER 8

I was flipping through a newspaper at the pool hall one day when I came across an ad for kickboxing lessons. To that point I'd been able to handle almost any situation I found myself in fairly well, but the fighting was starting to escalate, so I thought maybe some formal training would be a good idea. I signed up, and for the next year I attended classes twice a week. I was one of the quieter students, but I don't think I ever missed a session. I also practiced a lot on my own between classes. It was good conditioning, and I learned a few things about balance and technique. I enjoyed it and found that it came quite naturally. Often, while we were stretching out, I would look around and compare myself to the other guys in the class. I knew that if it ever came to a real fight I could take any one of them.

Johnboy and I kept hustling together, but more and more we started to go our separate ways. He thought I was getting too violent and taking too many chances. Along with that, little things we did and said were getting on each other's nerves. We were starting to drift apart.

At the pool hall I was getting to know a guy named Paul. He was a really nice, friendly guy, and I found out after a while that he was one of the leaders of the Baptist youth group I had gone to a couple of times a few years earlier. I started going back out to the Red Rock Roller Dome once in a while, and one evening the church youth group was out there, too. It wasn't a roller derby night; it was just public skating. There were a couple of guys out on the floor showing off, which didn't impress me, but when they knocked over Paul's sister I thought I should teach them a thing or two about proper etiquette. I skated over and set them down on their butts.

The leaders of the youth group were Harvey and Carol, a young couple who were expecting their first child in a few months. Harvey wasn't much of a skater, but when he saw that things were getting physical out on the floor he wobbled up behind me and grabbed me by the arm. I instantly spun around and dropped him with one shot to the face. When he hit the floor I landed on top of him and quickly fed him a few more. I hadn't even thought about what I was doing—it was just an automatic reaction. He was bleeding badly, and I could hear people screaming.

I went over to the side, quickly took off my skates, and Paul gave me a ride back to the pool hall. I heard later that Harvey had been taken to the hospital by ambulance. His nose had been rearranged, but other than that he was okay. But Carol had a miscarriage that night and they lost the baby. I felt terrible for what I had done.

The memory of that night plagued me for a long time. Three or four years later I called them up to apologize for what I had done, and they said they forgave me. They also said that God had blessed them with a beautiful, healthy child and they were now expecting their second one. I still felt bad, but I was glad that things were working out for them.

After the Roller Dome incident Paul kept coming around the pool hall and talking to me. He told me he was attending Berean Bible College in Calgary, and thought I should come with him for a semester. I didn't think that would work out very well, but he kept on telling me I should give it a try. I hadn't been to Calgary since Johnboy and I had beaten up a couple of guys with our pool cues and robbed them a few months earlier. But as I thought about it I decided I might be up for a bit of adventure. I also needed some time away from Johnboy. The semester was starting right away, but since I had to take care of a few things first I told Paul I would take the bus down there in a couple of weeks.

When I got to the bus station in Calgary the dean of students, Paul and the guy who was to be my roommate were there to meet me. I stepped off the bus wearing my buckskin jacket, hair down to my elbows, a knife strapped to the side of my boot and a much bigger knife hanging from my belt. I don't know what Paul had told them at the school, but it was immediately obvious that they were totally intimidated, and didn't have a clue what they were going to do with me.

I arrived on the weekend, and since there weren't any classes until Monday I decided to go down the road to the pool hall. I thought it was quite convenient having the pool hall that close to the school. When I walked in I immediately noticed a girl with raven black, curly hair. She looked to be a few years older than me, but she was the most beautiful thing I had ever seen. I asked around and found out her name was Brenda, and that she was known as the acid queen of Calgary. I was warned she was a dangerous girl to be around, and that sounded good to me.

There were already two other guys showing interest in her, so I went over to join the conversation. I told her I had just arrived in town and asked her to play some pool. The other guys joined us. While the four of us were playing, she pulled out a vial containing 100 tabs of acid. Between us, we did all 100 hits right there—probably the craziest thing I had ever done.

The pool hall was on the second floor of a three-storey building. One of the guys freaked out and ran out the exit and up to the roof. The other guy stumbled through the plate glass window, fell onto the parking lot below and, within a couple of minutes, was dead from his injuries. Brenda and I got out of there as fast as we could. We hid out for a while and then she invited me over to her place. I spent the next two weeks at her apartment partying, doing drugs and having sex.

The guys from the Bible school had no idea what had happened to me. They went out looking for me the first few nights and then decided maybe I had changed my mind and gone back home. When I showed up at school again, they didn't know what to think. I lived in the dorm for the next six weeks, but it was clear to everyone that this school wasn't for me. I attended a few classes, but I was high on acid and in a haze the whole time I was there. I couldn't understand a thing they were teaching, and even if I could have I had no intention of learning anything anyway. That's not what I was there for. For me it was just a change of scenery, and when I got bored with it I would move on to the next thing.

Besides, I figured this whole religion thing was just a scam. Everybody has a scam, and this was theirs. I had my way of surviving and they had theirs. I suppose I always believed there was something out there bigger than us, and when I looked around I knew that something had to have created all of this. I just never spent much time thinking about it. Sometimes when I did I hoped there was a God out there somewhere, yet other times I cursed the God that might be out there somewhere. Most of the time though I just didn't care.

When I ran out of things to do in Calgary I got back on the bus and went home to Prince George.

That spring Johnboy got a job at a grocery store and I started spending more time alone at the pool hall. One day when I came back to our motel room, he was having a party with a few of his friends from work. I told him the music was too loud and went to turn it down. He came over and gave me a little shove and told me to back off.

"Don't be stupid and push your luck," I said.

He picked up a couple of knives off the counter and started waving them around. "What are you going to do about it?" he asked.

I guess he thought his friends would step in and back him up, but no one moved. I punched him in the head a few times and then knocked him onto the couch and fed him a few more. That was the end of the party, and it was also the end of us. After that, I went out and rented a little room in a boarding house.

I kept playing pool, but I also started to hit the nightclubs after that. I loved the clubs. Nightclubs and I were like magic. I had turned 17 by then, but I was still too young to get in (you needed to be 18) so I lied about my age. Most often they knew I was lying, but everyone seemed to like me, and they never turned me away. Back in junior high I had done some DJ-ing at school dances, and I was quite good at it. After a while I started DJ-ing at some of the clubs, but my real love was bouncing. I was just a scrawny teenager, but I wasn't afraid of anyone. I could deal with anything that broke out, and I looked for any opportunity to fight. I loved it—the more violence, the better. I quickly got a reputation, and people learned to respect my abilities and not mess with me.

After working the nightclubs for a while I decided that maybe having an honest job wasn't so bad after all. So, I lied about my age again and went to work on the oil rigs. Rena's boyfriend was working there and got me on with his crew.

To get to the job site, we had to fly from Prince George into Alberta. When we were getting ready to head out the first morning the guy sitting next to me pointed to my feet and said, "It's going to be cold out there. You'd better put on two pairs of socks." Immediately I thought of what I had promised myself years ago while hiding from the police in the culvert. I smiled, and slipped on another pair of socks. From that day on I wore two pairs of socks, and still do today to remind myself where I've come from.

On the oil rigs we rotated our shifts two weeks in and one week out, but after I had done my first two weeks, the roughneck on the crew replacing us didn't show up, so I volunteered to stay on and take his place. After that, I just stayed on with my regular crew and worked another two-week rotation.

After working five straight weeks of 12-hour days, my paycheque was more money than I ever had before, legally. The crew boss was a good man, and because he knew I would just go back home and blow it all, he offered to hold some of it back for me. I told him what I thought of that idea, and headed for home with a full five week's pay in my pocket. I blew every penny of it. I bought a waterbed and a stereo, and the rest of it went for drugs and booze. A week later I borrowed $100 from Rena to buy a plane ticket to get back to work.

After a few more shifts on the rigs I decided I needed a bigger place to live, so I rented a townhouse. I told Rena that if she moved in with me and did the housework I would pay the rent and look after all the expenses. That way I wouldn't have to worry about anything, and could just spend my time partying whenever I came home. The arrangement worked out well for both of us. She was the responsible one who appreciated having a place to live rent-free, and I just wanted to get high and party and not have any responsibilities or worries.

I kept hustling at the pool hall whenever I was back in Prince George, but over time I started spending more time at the nightclubs. The money was better there, and I just loved the nightlife. I loved everything about the clubs—the fighting, the music, the dancing—I loved it all. I was bringing home different girls all the time. Life for me was all about drugs, sex and fighting, when necessary. That's all I cared about.

For a few years already I had been selling drugs on the side, but now I started to get into dealing more seriously. I found I could easily turn an investment of a few hundred

Rena and me. I'm 17 years old

dollars into a few thousand dollars, sometimes in just one night. I was making more money than ever, and it was all going into drugs and partying. A few guys from the oil rigs started coming home with me on our week off, and we would spend the whole week in Prince George hitting the clubs, partying, drinking and doing drugs. I was spending thousands of dollars on drugs, sometimes in a single day.

I had been working on the rigs for about a year when the tip of my finger got caught in a chain one day, and was cut off at the last knuckle. The doctor was able to sew it back on, but I was off work for the next couple of months. After the finger healed I really didn't feel like going back, because I was enjoying the nightclubs too much. And besides, I was making good money hustling and selling drugs, so I thought I would just stay with that for a while.

Allan, a buddy of mine from the nightclub who worked as a bucker for a logging crew, moved in with me and the partying just went nuts. We did a few road trips together, just throwing a bunch of drugs into the car and heading to Edmonton for some action—sort of like taking the party on the road. We stayed good friends for the next three or four years, but eventually we went our separate ways when a cute girl came along and swept Allan off his feet. Besides, my life of drugs, girls, partying and violence all eventually got to the point where it was just too out of control for him.

Rena had been able to put up with the partying every third week when I was home from the rigs, but now that it was going non-stop it was too much for her, and she moved out.

Honestly, I knew I couldn't just party my life away, so one day I applied for work at the BC Rail office in town when I saw they were hiring. I got a job doing survey work for spur lines, and immediately loved it, especially because the hours were perfect: 5 days a week from 8 to 4, with weekends off. Our crew of three worked mostly near Prince George, and occasionally out of town for a week.

My life fell into a predictable routine for the next few months. Every day after work I would go home and smoke a joint, and then nap for a few hours. Around 7:30 I would get cleaned up and then hit the clubs until 3:00 or 4:00 a.m. Then I'd crawl into bed for a few hours' sleep until my boss pulled up at 8:00 a.m. He'd honk his horn until I got up and waved at him from my bedroom window, and then he'd drive down to the corner gas station, pick up a couple of coffees and come back for me 10 minutes later. Then while we drove to work we'd smoke a joint together and listen to the radio.

Our crew always got our work done, but not without smoking a lot of pot and doing a lot of goofing around. I'd say we spent just as much time getting high and laughing as we did working. During the six months I worked there I turned 19.

Back when I was working on the oil rigs I had started to get into a pretty serious relationship with a girl in Prince George. She ended up getting pregnant, and during the time I worked for the railway our son, Jason Lee, was born. I insisted his second name be Lee, after the martial arts fighter, Bruce Lee. I loved our little son, and I began to see the world differently, now that I was a father. I started to take a bit more responsibility, and although I was still drinking heavily and doing crazy amounts of drugs, I vowed that my son would never be wanting for anything. I would look after him and make sure he had everything he needed. I would be a real father—not the kind of father my dad had been.

Jason's mother was a partier like me, but I was still too wild for her, so the relationship really didn't go anywhere. She and Jason lived with her parents (who didn't like me at all), but she allowed me take to Jason sometimes. When I did I would usually take him down to the pool hall to show him off.

A few months later while I was out with the survey crew, the police came for me with some bad news. My son had died. No one knew exactly what had happened. He had gone to sleep in his crib and at some time during the night he just stopped breathing.

I was a wreck. I had been trying to get my life together, and could see a future for myself—I had even started to feel this thing called love. But all that had been wiped out in one cruel blow. After the funeral I wandered around in a daze for a couple of hours, and then went out to the cemetery to spend the night at the grave of my son.

I quit my job after that, and for the next few months my life went into a tailspin. I started doing even more drugs. I didn't care what I was doing to my mind or my body. I just did whatever I could to escape the pain. There was so much cocaine going through my system that sometimes my friends didn't even want to be around me. I was a mess.

That summer Allan and I moved out of the townhouse and rented a big, five-bedroom house together with three other guys. It became nothing but a party house, where people came every night to drink and do drugs all night long. Our rule was that no one could come in unless they brought a bottle of whiskey. After a couple of months we had created a pyramid of

Behind me is the beginning of the pyramid of empty bottles

literally hundreds of empty bottles piled up against the living room wall.

The house was four blocks from the nightclub, and The Happy Face Restaurant was in between. One night at the restaurant, four of us spent a few hours ordering meals, drinks, desserts—anything we felt like eating. Then, when we were so stuffed that we couldn't eat any more, someone yelled "go" and we all jumped up and ran out without paying. We could have easily paid the bill, because money wasn't a problem, but we just didn't feel like it. It was just a big joke to us. We did the same thing a couple more times over the next while (sometimes even asking for separate bills), with as many as 13 guys around the table. The owner chased us for a little while, but I don't think he really wanted to catch any of us too badly. We were bad news.

It was common knowledge around town that I was a drug dealer. I knew the police were watching our house and keeping an eye on me at the nightclubs where I did most of my business, so I knew I had to be careful. It became a kind of cat-and-mouse game, with me quietly selling hundreds of hits of speed every night at the clubs, and they just waiting for the right moment to nab me with enough drugs in my possession to put me away for a while.

One evening at our house we noticed police cruisers parked at both ends of the block. There was a lot of drugs in the place, so we were afraid they had us surrounded and were getting ready to make their move. Some of the other guys in the house were getting nervous, but I told them to relax because I had a plan. I called a cab company to send seven cabs to our address—one cab for each of us— and told them to make sure the cabs all arrived at exactly the same time. I explained to the guys that when the cabs arrived we would all run out and jump into separate cars, and tell the cabbies to quickly take off in different directions. As we were leaving we'd duck down in the back seats so the police couldn't see us.

The plan worked like a charm. It all happened so fast that in all the confusion the police didn't know what to do or who to pull over. We met up later that night at a club and had a good laugh about it.

A couple of weeks later I was standing outside a bar one day smoking a joint, and watching a stone mason working on a new hotel complex being built next door. There was a lot of elaborate stonework going into the front of the building, which I thought looked kind of interesting. I went over and started visiting with the guy, and found out his name was also Richard. After we talked for a while he offered me a job, and for the next couple of months I helped him finish up the work on the hotel, called Esther's Inn. Our work can still be seen there today.

He paid me $400 a week cash under the table. At the same time I was also making $14 an hour at the nightclub, which was a pretty good wage back then. But my best source of income was still selling drugs—300 to 500 Bennies (speed) a night at $3 each or two for $5. The product, imported from the States through the postal system, was costing me only about 10 cents a pop, so I was getting a fairly good return on my investment.

One evening in the pool hall I noticed a couple of guys, who I guessed to be a few years older than me, looking over at me and sizing me up. After a while they came over and challenged me to a game of pool. They were trying to hustle me, but as it turned out I hustled a few dollars off them. They didn't want to pay, so I took my pool cue apart and hit one of them a few times. They started acting tough, but when they saw that I wasn't backing down they left pretty quickly.

After they were gone another guy who had been with them came over and asked, "Do you know who those guys are?" I told him I didn't.

"They're martial arts students," he said.

I didn't think anything more about it until about a week later when a little Oriental man came into the pool hall asking for me. He wanted to meet this scrawny teenager who had beaten up one of his students, who weren't supposed to be fighting. They really hadn't—they had backed off quickly—but he had heard them talking about me, and was curious to find out who I was.

His name was Tuny, and as he spoke in his strong Oriental accent I immediately respected him; he seemed like the most humble, gentle man I had ever met. He invited me to his studio later that week to, as he put it, "channo' tha' enogy."

The studio was in a single-storey building that looked to me like an old dance hall. The moment I walked in I knew this was where I belonged. The dressing rooms were on the right, and beyond them was all sorts of martial arts training equipment and gear along the wall. The rest of the wall was mirror, from floor to ceiling. In the back corner along the opposite wall were several sizes of heavy punching bags. All over the studio at various heights were 6" x 12" rubber mats sticking out from the walls at 90° angles. I was impressed by what I saw, and I hoped this guy could teach me something.

There were about 16 students in the marital arts class. I figured I was the youngest one there, other than one kid who looked to be about 13. I was just wearing sweatpants and running shoes, so Tuny told me to put on a Gi. One of the guys showed me how to wear it and how to tie the belt up properly while the other guys lined up and did some stretching. I went to the back of the room by the big bags and fell in line. Tuny stood in front of the mirrored wall, and everyone spread out in a couple of rows facing him. I just watched and did what everyone else was doing.

We began by stretching every tendon and joint in our body, moving from the top of our heads right down to our toes. We rolled our eyes, flexed our jaw and loosened every joint. I was used to stretching out my muscles, but this was new to me. Only after we had completely limbered up did we begin to stretch out our muscles.

Watching the other students stretch, I could tell I had more flexibility than anyone there. I could kick higher, do the splits better and was quicker than any of them. I thought to myself, "I'm at the top of this class. I have more rage and ugliness inside of me than any of these guys, plus I've got more skill too!" By the time we finished stretching out I was starting to feel pretty cocky.

Most of the guys were wearing different coloured belts. I had a white belt, which didn't impress me very much. I decided the guys with the black belts were the ones I wanted to spar with. I recognized the guy I had roughed up in the pool hall, wearing a blue belt.

By now I was sweating pretty good. We were all barefoot, which I wasn't used to doing, being a street fighter. You always kept your shoes on to use as weapons.

Tuny got us doing some leg thrusts. Again, I watched what the other guys were doing and tried to follow along. They were bringing their knees up to their chests and then kicking their legs out. I knew I could kick higher and harder than any of them, so I lifted my knee and shot my leg out as fast as I could, except I got a little more thrust than I was expecting. My bare foot slipped off the floor and I landed flat on my back with a loud thud. I was embarrassed, but more than that, I was mad, and bounced back up even faster than I had gone down. I immediately spun around, started swearing and then exploded into the bag behind me. I gave the bag a few good shots while I was cursing and yelling, and then turned around and faced the front again.

You could have heard a pin drop. After the kick you're supposed to get back into your stance, but everyone was just standing there, staring at me. Tuny looked at me for a couple of seconds, shook his head in bewilderment, and then went on with the lesson like nothing had happened.

A little later in the session he told us to line up facing a partner, so I ran over to one of the black belt guys and stood in front of him. Tuny came over and told me to go line up with someone else.

I'm not sure what the other guys thought of me, but I loved that first session. It was amazing! I felt like I was made for this. The moves seemed to almost come naturally to me. I decided that evening I would make the most of this, and I would learn everything I could from Tuny.

Tuny, I found out, was well-known in martial arts circles and had even worked with some big-name Hollywood actors. His classes were Tuesday and Thursday evenings for two hours, with an optional class on Sunday afternoons. From that first day on I almost never missed a class. I was there three times a week, and loved every minute of it. The classes were always over way too soon for me. I just wanted to keep going.

After a couple of weeks, Tuny called me aside after class one day and told me he wanted to start doing some extra work with me, to become his special protégé. "You have specio' gift," he said. "You have lots of enogy, but enogy that needs to be channo'd."

That sounded good to me. I had found something I loved, and I couldn't get enough of it. From then on I started getting more of his attention in the evening classes, and stayed around after so he could work with me one-on-one. He told me over and over again that a special gift like mine shouldn't be wasted. He also tried to impress upon me that it shouldn't be abused.

Besides working with me in the studio, he started inviting me over to his house. His back yard was incredible! There were some big trees behind his house, and hanging from the branches were all sorts of apparatuses. There were different sizes of punching bags and heavy rubber mats that he had made from old conveyor belts. They were hanging at various heights and on different lengths of rope so that when you hit them they would swing back at you at different speeds and from every possible angle. On the trunks of the trees were attached more rubber mats all the way from ground level to over my head. I would go out there and punch, kick, spin and duck. He would watch and then give me some instructions and show me what to do. Then I'd go at it again. I would spend hours out there refining my technique, learning how to defend myself from whatever was coming at me, and becoming skilled in using every part of my body as a weapon.

One of the simplest but most amazing workout tools Tuny introduced me to was the wheel, which was just an eight-inch wheel with a short handle on either side. He showed me how to get down on the floor in a push-up position and then grip the wheel handles, holding myself up while rolling the wheel back and forth in front of me. It was incredibly hard to do, and at first I couldn't do more than just a few rotations at a time. I worked hard at it though, and after a while I had built up enough strength in my arms and torso that I could fully extend myself and keep rolling back and forth for quite a while without stopping. I learned to not just extend straight forward, but to also roll from side to side. It was great for working on balance, but most of all it built up and firmed the muscles in my torso. The torso generates both the speed and the power that are needed in fighting, and as I used the wheel I could literally feel my muscles becoming hardened.

I was still working regular day hours doing stonework with Richard, keeping quite busy on fireplaces, mostly. It was hard physical work, but I liked that. And I had my evenings off to play pool, hit the clubs, party and attend martial arts classes.

Teaching martial arts was just a sideline for Tuny. He spent his days working as the produce manager at a grocery store. He was always interested in what I did for work, and kept asking about it. Finally, one day he said he was tired of the grocery business and wanted to start working for himself, so he was going to buy out my boss's business. Over the next couple of months an agreement was reached, and Tuny became my new boss at Sunshine Fireplaces.

Most of our work was in Prince George, so at noon each day we would take an hour off and go back to his house for lunch. Every day it was the same thing—I would work out in the back yard, and he would stand by his kitchen window, cooking noodles and yelling out instructions and encouragement. Then, while we ate, he would tell me what he saw and how I could improve my technique. I was a raw fighter, and he was a technician—an artist. He taught me the art of fighting, how to use my feet like hands and to anticipate and then react with lightning speed and agility to whatever was coming at me.

After working with me for six months he told me that if I was in a competition being judged on form and technique, I would probably lose. But if it ever came down to raw rage and fighting until only one man was left standing I was in a league of my own. He told me no one would stand a chance against me.

We were working together on a fireplace one day when he told me he had a taekwondo master coming to the studio from Calgary to give a demonstration that evening. "He going to ask for volunteer," Tuny said, "and when he ask, you don't volunteer."

I nodded.

Tuny stopped what he was doing, looked at me and said again, slowly and sternly, "You don't volunteer!" He shook his finger at me.

I nodded.

For the rest of the day all I could think about was how good it was going to feel to take out that taekwondo master. I could hardly wait for class to start. The other students didn't know he'd be asking for a volunteer, but I was ready and waiting. As soon as I heard the words, "I need..." my hand shot into the air. Tuny just shook his head and looked away.

I stepped forward and the taekwondo master said a few words of explanation and then made a move towards me. I was poised and ready, and as soon as I saw him move I kicked him in the groin so hard that he dropped to the mat and lay there groaning. He couldn't go on, and the rest of the demonstration had to be cancelled.

I trained full-time with Tuny for the next two-and-a-half years, until I left Prince George. During that time my fighting was raised to a level that I would have never dreamed possible.

I had no concept of life without fighting and violence—fighting had been my life, right from the start. From all that I had been through I had learned to read body language and know how and when people were going to respond. The way someone swallows, or shifts his feet, or positions his body, or flinches or tenses his muscles are all giveaways, telling me what's coming. That knowledge had literally been beaten into me. Now I was becoming a finely-tuned machine. The rage inside me, my natural speed and agility, the proficiency at defending myself that I learned from being beaten countless times, my ability to withstand incredible levels of pain, and now the training I was getting from Tuny all combined to make me into an awesome and lethal fighting machine.

My martial arts training also took my dancing to the next level. As a little kid I had natural rhythm, moving to the country music always playing in our house. Sometimes Doris would catch me dancing and ridicule me, but it didn't stop me. The movement seemed to come naturally. I even had a little toy guitar I would play while I sang along to the songs when no one was around, until Doris caught me one day and smashed my guitar. Still, I loved to dance, and kept it up whenever I could.

Now my martial arts moves started to show up on the dance floor. I started to incorporate the kicks and spins I was learning into my dancing. I loved the limelight, and when it was show time I could turn it on. Anything with movement came naturally to me.

On a club dance floor

I won a couple of local dance competitions, and got my picture in the paper a few times. When I advanced to the regional competitions I won them, too. I was starting to get quite a reputation as a dancer. One day a local cable TV station asked if I'd be interested in co-hosting a Saturday morning dance show, and I said I'd give it a try. It was a live show, with people on the dance floor and others watching from the stands. My co-host was a beautiful blond girl, who later went on to star in a popular TV soap opera. We lived together for a few months while doing the show, but the drugs and partying were too intense for her, and the relationship didn't last. After six months of hosting, I was finding it too hard to get to the studio on time on Saturday mornings, and finally quit.

While I was hosting the show, a few club owners in town hired me as a dance instructor, also paying me commission for everyone I could get to sign up for dance lessons. It worked out quite well. I'd take the ladies out on the floor, make them feel like they could dance, and then chat them up to sign a two-year contract. I quickly found out I was a smooth talker and could talk almost anyone into signing on.

After I'd signed up everyone I could in Prince George, they took me down to the States for a couple of months where they had partners in Oregon wanting me to do the same thing for them. While I was there they put me up in a nice chalet and gave me everything I wanted—money, drugs and women—I was living a crazy life. I found myself doing a lot more cocaine, just to keep my energy up. I might have stayed there longer, but after a couple months I got myself into some trouble and had to head back to Prince George.

A buddy and I started running drugs between Prince George and Vancouver as a little side business. On one of the runs, as I was clipping along at a pretty good pace in a Trans Am (which my buddy had just won in a poker game), we went through a speed trap a few miles outside Williams Lake. We knew it wouldn't be in our best interest to stop since we had a car full of drugs, so I hit the gas and got going up to around 100 mph. As we crested the hill about a mile before the town we saw that a road block had been set up in an attempt to discourage us from going any further. There was a fire truck and a couple of police cars parked across the highway. I knew from my days with BC Rail that the rail yard ran right through town, and by going through the yard we could avoid the roadblock. I pulled off the highway and into the rail yard, still going close to 100 mph. When the car hit the tracks I lost control and we started to flip. The police told us later that, by their count, we had rolled 13 times. There were pieces of the car spread out all over the place.

It was a miracle we walked out of that one. My buddy had a cut on his forehead, but other than a few bruises, that was the only injury either of us sustained. The police were so stunned that we walked away from the crash that they didn't even charge us. They didn't know we were running drugs; they were just pulling us over for speeding. I guess they figured that losing the car was enough punishment, so they let us walk. We sold what was left of the car to the tow truck driver for $50 and took the bus out of town. The drugs were a complete loss. The crash had spread them out all over the rail yard.

Later that summer we won a Corvette in another poker game. We were playing for pretty high stakes, but to us it wasn't much of a risk. We were starting to make enough money selling and running drugs that it wasn't hard to cover any losses we might incur. On one of our drug runs we took the Corvette into Victoria to street race along Douglas St. in front of the Greyhound bus depot. A Chevy 4x4 truck pulled out in front of us and we T-boned it, so that was the end of the Corvette. We totaled off two pretty nice cars that summer.

I was spending all my time dancing, partying, fighting, selling drugs and trying to avoid the police. It was a lot of fun, but I knew that my life was out of control, and that something needed to change. I was getting too crazy for my friends who were starting to stay away, and I couldn't stay in a relationship with any girl I liked. I felt like I was being ripped apart inside. I was having fun, but along with it there was a growing emptiness that nothing seemed to fill. There was too much pain, too many memories. I had to move on.

Terry, a guy I knew from the nightclubs who owned a drywall business, said he was heading to Elkford in southeastern B.C. where things were booming, and invited me to come along to work for him. I told him yes. A few days later I visited my son's grave one last time, and then said goodbye to Tuny and my friends, leaving Prince George for good.

CHAPTER 9

Terry and I landed a couple of drywall jobs right away in Elkford, and went to work. Elkford was a change of scenery for me, but not much else in my life changed. We stayed in a hotel, with not much else to do after work except go to the bars. I couldn't seem to avoid fighting. I had enough of an attitude to get the people around me mad, and I never backed down from anyone. The Fording Coal Mining Company was the biggest employer in the region, and the miners had a reputation of being a rough bunch. They were used to running roughshod over the town and the nightclubs, so when I showed up on the scene there was definitely potential for conflict. It wasn't long before more than pleasantries were being exchanged, and after I had laid out a couple of guys word got around, and most people either left me alone or backed down quickly.

I was a hard worker, and although I had never done any drywall work before I caught on quickly. On those first few jobs we made good money—maybe a little too good. Terry had agreed to give me 40% of the profits, but while sitting in the bar after finishing the second job he said he had decided 30% would be more appropriate. I told him what he could do with that idea. He handed me some cash and said that's all I would be getting, and I told him he had better hand over the rest of what he owed me.

"I've been doing this for a lot of years, and I've never paid anyone as much as I'm paying you," he said.

"That's because you've never had anyone who works as hard as me," I shot back. "Now give me the rest of it!"

We argued back and forth for a while, and I made sure it got loud enough for everyone sitting nearby to hear what was going on. Finally, I punched him in the head, knocking him out. While he lay there I reached into his pocket, pulled out his wad of cash, counted out what he owed me and then threw the rest on the table. Everyone in the bar was staring at me. I looked around and said, "You saw how he was trying to rip me off—I'm just taking what's mine." I turned and walked out.

The next day I was standing around, waiting for the bar to open and wondering what to do next. I was unemployed, but I was quite sure I would come up with something. Just then I saw a Loomis armoured truck parked across the street at the Royal Bank. One of the guards was standing at the back of the truck having a smoke while the other one went into the building with what I assumed was the payroll for the mining company. As I watched them I started thinking about how easy it would be to make the biggest score of my life. It looked like a pretty straightforward job, and to this day I still think I could have pulled it off. I don't know if I actually would have gotten away with it, but I could have taken both of them out so fast they would have never known what had happened.

As I stood there looking over the situation a guy walked in front of me, slowly pushing a wheelbarrow full of mortar over to a stonemason working on the shopping mall next door. I looked back and forth between the Loomis truck and the guy pushing the wheelbarrow. It struck me as an odd contrast. Who knew how many thousands of dollars were in that truck? But I had worked for a stonemason before, and didn't mind the work. I stood there for several minutes, trying to make up my mind. I had a strange feeling I was at a crossroads in my life. Did I want to go to work, or rob the truck? I wasn't sure.

I chuckled out loud, thinking how ironic and kind of funny it was that the wheelbarrow had rolled past at that exact moment. It seemed really weird. I finally decided it was too much of a coincidence to ignore.

I walked up to the guy pushing the wheelbarrow. He looked kind of lazy to me. I lit a joint and smoked it with him while I asked about his job, how much he was making an hour and what his boss was like. After talking for a few minutes I thanked him for the information and then told him I was going to take his job. I found his boss and told him I could work 10 times faster than that lazy so-and-so he had working for him now. "Give me one day," I said, "and I'll prove it to you." He looked me over and then looked over at his worker, slowly dawdling along with the wheelbarrow. He wasn't quite sure what to think.

"I'll tell you what," I said. "Give that guy the day off tomorrow, and I'll come work for you. If you're not happy with me, you can give him my wages for the day and nobody's out anything."

He watched his worker for a few more seconds, shook his head and yelled to him, "You got the day off tomorrow!" I showed up first thing next morning, and made sure I stayed ahead of the boss all day long. He never had to wait for mud even once. He never called the other guy back.

I spent the next few months working for George. He was from Lethbridge, Alberta, and had come to Elkford that summer to make some extra money for a new house he was building back home. At the end of the summer he asked me to come with him to finish his house. I didn't have anything else to do, and I couldn't see much of a future for myself in Elkford, so I went with him.

I started hitting the pool hall as soon as we got to Lethbridge, and it didn't take me long to realize that it was a gold mine. I had never seen money like that in a pool hall. The oil business was booming, and the guys coming in from the rigs had wallets that were bulging with cash. George and I finished up his house in a couple of weeks, and after that I got a job with a roofer for a short while. But when I realized the kind of money I could make at the pool hall I quit that job, too. I was making hundreds, and sometimes even thousands, of dollars a night hustling and playing pool. Most of that money went straight into drugs and booze.

I was staying in a motel right across the street from a 24-hour Mr. Sub shop. The first thing I noticed about it was the absolutely gorgeous girl working behind the counter. The sub shop was a father-and-son operation, and it didn't take me long to figure out that the son was selling more than just sandwiches. He wasn't too smart about it, though; he ended up selling dope to the wrong undercover cop and got sent to prison for five years.

After he was gone, things got interesting. There were three bars along the same street that were open until 3:00 a.m., and after closing time some of the less desirable clientele would come around to Mr. Sub. Not all of them realized the son had been busted, so they still came looking for drugs. A pretty girl and a bunch of upset drunks is never a good combination, and I noticed a few times that things were getting a little out of hand.

I was looking for an opportunity to get to know the girl, so I thought that perhaps if I went over there and demonstrated what I could do, she might be impressed. Since leaving Prince George nearly a year earlier I hadn't been doing any problem-solving. I had actually kept a pretty low profile in Elkford, and other than a few fights in the pool hall, I hadn't really done much in Lethbridge, either. But I could see how my services could be put to use in this situation.

After I'd gone over there a couple of times and taken care of a few goofs who were out of line, it was the owner, Terry, who was impressed. He asked me if I'd be willing to hang around the place and settle things down. That was all the invitation I needed. I had to do something besides just play pool.

I started working the afternoon shift at the sub shop the next day. Making sandwiches for people was a new experience for me, but I kind of enjoyed it. I liked interacting with people, and the schedule was great for me. I'd work an afternoon shift at the sub shop, hit the pool hall and bars in the evenings, work the night shift at the sub shop, sleep all morning, and then get up after lunch to start it all over. I knew by now how to make the right connections, so it wasn't long before I was controlling the drug trade in that area of town.

After a couple of weeks at the sub shop, I noticed an old man coming around every night, looking through the garbage can in the parking lot. A few times I saw him pull out a piece of leftover sandwich and eat it. I felt sorry for him, so one night I ran out and gently slapped his hand while he was lifting out a sandwich piece, but this scared him. I felt really bad about it, so I told him I just wanted him to come inside so I could make him a fresh sandwich.

He struggled with English through his eastern European accent, but he made it clear that he wasn't going to accept my charity. "No, no, no," he said, shaking his head. "No take." He was a proud man—I instantly respected him.

I noticed that he was coming around every morning at 2:00, so I started putting a fresh six-inch sub in the garbage can just before he got there, making sure to rough up the wrapper so it looked like someone had thrown it away. I knew he would realize I was putting it there for him, but I wanted to protect his dignity.

This had been going on for a few months when one night four mouthy punks came into the shop, right about the time that I needed to put out the old man's sub. I was trying to rush through their order, but there were a few other people waiting too, and I was getting a bit behind. I kept looking at the clock, realizing that I wasn't going to get out there in time. I was just finishing up their order when I saw the old man walk over and look into the garbage. I felt terrible for him, and was mad at the punks. They were acting like jerks, causing the old man to miss his supper.

I had just turned to help the next customer when I heard one of them say, "Hey, there's that old man. Let's go rob him again."

When I heard the word "again" I instantly felt the hair on the back of my neck stand on end. I watched them head out the door and go around the corner of the building in the direction that the old man had gone. "Watch my till!" I yelled to the customer in the front of the line as I jumped over the counter and ran out the door after them. When I caught up to them in the back alley, they already had the old man up against the building. One of them was holding him by his neck, and the others were going through his pockets. I flew into the guy holding the old man, breaking the guy's arm, and then grabbed two of his buddies. The fourth one ran away like a coward. He was willing to beat up an old man together with his buddies, but he didn't want anything to do with me. After beating the three of them up pretty good, I went through their pockets and found a total of $60. I made the guy with the broken arm apologize to the old man and give him the money.

But the old man didn't want to take it. In fact, while I was beating up the three guys he had been telling me to stop. "No hurt. No hurt," he kept saying. So, other than the broken arm, I let them go with nothing more than a few good bruises. It would have been a lot worse, but I wanted to respect the old man. Before I let them go I told them I would be watching, and if I ever saw as much as a scratch on the old man I wouldn't try to find out how he got it—I would just find them and break every bone in their bodies. They seemed to get the message.

For the next few years the old man kept coming around, and I put a sandwich out for him every night.

After a while I moved out of the hotel and moved in with a couple of girls I had gotten to know. I was hitting the nightclubs again, making a name for myself as a hustler, dancer and fighter. The girls invited me to move in with them and again we just partied the days away. We were high all the time.

But the living arrangement didn't work out for very long. The girls started fighting with each other, and then started fighting with me when I brought other girls home. I knew I had to get out of there, so I asked Terry if I could move into the basement of the sub shop. It was just a big empty room, with nothing more than a small office and a bathroom. He didn't see a problem with me living there, so I bought a bed and some other furniture, and moved in. For the next two-and-a-half years that was home. I thought it was great—everything I needed was right there within a couple of blocks.

I knew that if I was going to be a serious fighter I had to keep honing my skills. So I put mirrors on the walls of my basement apartment and hung heavy bags, double-end bags and speed bags from the ceiling. There were a couple of old framed doors that had been put in storage down in the basement, so I put them to good use, too. On one door I painted the outline of a person holding a knife, and on the other door a person holding a gun. I used them for target practice with my throwing stars, steel darts and knives. I didn't just aim for the doors; I practiced precision throwing—taking out a wrist, a knee or an eye. With my knife I would sometimes aim for the heart. I practiced throwing for hours at a time, and after I while I never missed the exact spot I was aiming for. I didn't even have to think about what I was doing. I would go from the bags to the throwing stars and knives and back to the bags again in one fluid motion, without missing a beat. I also kept working out with the wheel, like Tuny taught me. I wanted to keep my whole body hardened and toned.

I didn't just work on the physical elements. I had learned from Tuny that the mental part of being a fighter was even more important than the physical, so I worked at honing my skills in all the senses.

I would sometimes sit for long periods of time, doing nothing except listening to the sounds around me. I would close my eyes and focus on every sound, trying to picture what it was and where it was coming from. I got to the point where I could shut my eyes and listen to a fly buzzing around the room and then reach out and snatch it when it came within reach. That's done in the movies all the time now, but I was already doing it long before I ever saw in on the screen.

I did the same thing with my sense of smell. I tried to become acutely aware of every aroma around me. What was it? What was making it? Where was it coming from? How many different smells could I identify at the same time? This wasn't easy to do because my nose was in bad shape from being broken so many times.

I learned to do the splits while balancing between two chairs. I trained myself to hold that position for several minutes at a time while not consciously thinking about it. I would think about something else and let my subconscious do the balancing and flexing of the muscles in order to hold my position.

I worked on my alertness by staring straight ahead, not moving my head or my eyes. While staring at what was in front of me I would concentrate on what was happening on the farthest extent of my peripheral vision. I was trying to become completely in tune with everything happening around me. The more aware I was of my surroundings, the more prepared I would be for whatever situation I had to deal with. The more naturally and easily that awareness came about, the more energy I could focus on doing what needed to be done.

After living for a while in the basement, I brought a PacMan machine and then a juke box into the sub shop. They generated a bit more income for me, and since they hadn't exactly been obtained legally, there weren't any records to keep. It was all tax-free income.

The money was starting to come in quite well, so in the fall of 1983 I bought a brand new Ford Bronco II. I ordered it with every option available, and had it pimped out right from the factory—the only thing I added myself was a huge set of speakers. At night I would pull it up to the back doors of the sub shop, open the hatch, and crank the music. We'd party and play PacMan until the owners of the businesses next door would open up the next morning. There was a hair salon on one side and a men's clothing store on the other. The owners both loved me because as long as I was around there weren't any problems, kind of like having a security guard. We made a lot of noise, but I didn't want the police coming around, so I made sure that there wasn't any trouble.

There was a lot of money in town. The oil business was booming all over Alberta in the '80s, and it seemed that people had more money than they knew what to do with. Lots of money meant lots of drugs and violence, which couldn't have been more perfect for me.

The pool hall and the nightclub were side by side. That also couldn't have worked out any better for me. After a while I took over the drug trade at both places. I ruled my own corner of town, and no one messed with me.

In the nightclub I got paid $50 a fight working as a cooler (someone who quashes problems). Anytime someone got out of hand or a fight broke out, the manager would give me the nod, and I would go and deal with it. I never hesitated taking on four or five guys at once, if that's what the situation called for. I could handle whatever came at me, and the carnage I left behind was sometimes ugly. Anyone who tried to challenge me got hurt badly. If it was a quiet night and I was getting bored, or if I needed a little extra cash, I sometimes got a few of my buddies to start something. I loved it. I just danced and partied all night long, and fought whenever I was called on.

Besides taking care of any trouble at the nightclub, certain individuals started asking me again to take care of their problems. Debts needed collecting and scores needed settling. I had the willingness and the skills required to get the jobs done, sometimes dealing with some pretty big players, which was okay with me. The bigger the problem, the bigger the payout.

Several groups and organizations tried to recruit me into their "family," but I refused to align myself with anyone. I wanted to be free to call my own shots and to decide which jobs I wanted to do. I didn't want to have to bow down to anyone. And it wasn't just about the money—I didn't do jobs that were only about getting revenge or that would hurt people who were innocent, in my mind. But when an injustice had been done or when violence needed to be answered with violence, I was your man.

I usually carried a gun with me on my jobs, especially when I knew that the people I would be dealing with had guns, but I never had to use it. I sometimes threatened people with it, but I never fired a shot. Several times I had a gun pulled on me, but I was always able to either talk my way out of the situation or get within striking distance and disable the person. My weapons were my martial arts training, my mental alertness and my gift for fighting. I would only think of using a gun as a last resort to save my life.

My reputation as a fighter started to spread beyond Lethbridge. People started showing up from other cities, sometimes far away, just to fight me. They heard I was some sort of martial arts fighter, and they came to test their skills against me, or else they just wanted to prove they were the toughest thing around. I fought them all, never losing a fight.

I never hesitated to take on two, three, or even four guys at once, knowing I could handle whatever they threw at me. The fights were almost always over within a matter of seconds. When the fight involved more than one person I always threw them in a pile on top of each other when I was done with them. Leaving a pile of bodies stacked up behind me became my trademark.

I had my pick of just about any girl I wanted. I was controlling the drug trade in my corner of town, fighting whenever the situation called for it, and partying every night. I was a bad boy and a playboy, and the girls loved it. There were always plenty of opportunities to bring home a pretty lady for the evening. The girls from the rich side of town would invite me over to their place, and I accepted their offers quite often. If there was a pool table in the house then, after we'd had our fun, I would call up my buddies to come play pool until the sun came up. I took what the girls were offering, but I had no interest in having a relationship with any of them. I wanted my freedom. I didn't want to be tied down in any way.

I was having a lot of fun—I cannot deny it—but at the same time there was still an emptiness inside that kept gnawing away at me. Fighting felt good because it was a way of releasing some of that pent-up rage, but the ugliness that came out sometimes scared me. Drugs helped me escape to a place where I felt no pain, but it only lasted for a while and then the pain came back. I also I knew I was sinking further and further into hardcore drug addiction. I didn't like what I was doing to my body, but I felt like there was nothing I could do about it.

One afternoon while looking after some customers in the sub shop the phone rang, and I answered.

A man's voice said, "Hey Rocky, do you love me?"

I thought it was some kind of a joke. "Who is this?" I asked.

"It's Dean, your brother," he said. It took a few seconds to register, and then I remembered Dean had stayed with us for a while, way back when I was still a kid living with Doris. There were a lot of screwed-up relationships in our family, so I was never sure if Dean was my brother or my uncle. There was incest, kids from several different partners, and half-brothers and half-sisters from both my mom and dad. I couldn't say if Dean was my mom's brother or my brother.

"I just want to know if you love me," he said.

"Of course I do," I said.

There was a pause, and then he said, "I just wanted to know that somebody loved me before I checked out." I didn't even have time to respond. Right after he finished those words I heard the explosion of a shotgun blast. He had pulled the trigger.

I dropped the phone, jumped over the counter and ran the two blocks to the police station and told them that someone had just shot himself. By the time they tracked down the call the reports were already coming in. Dean had blown his head off in the bedroom while his wife and kids were sitting in the next room.

It shook me up and confused me. I wondered what kind of inner pain someone would need to be in to do that. It didn't make any sense that he would call me. I was angry that he would do that to his wife and kids, and angry that he had brought me into it.

When I think about it even now, I can still hear that shotgun going off. I have never been able to figure out why, of all the people he could have phoned, he called me. Maybe because he had seen first-hand the pain and hurt I had lived through as a child he thought I could somehow understand his pain. I don't know.

Life went on for me, and I continued to make a name for myself in Lethbridge. Some of the fights I got into were vicious, and people got hurt badly. There was one big brute of a man, about six-and-a-half feet tall and around 280 lbs, that I locked horns with a few times. There was something about him that was beyond any kind of evil I had ever encountered. I had been around a lot of bad characters, but he was in a league of his own. Whenever I was close to him the hair on the back of my neck stood on end.

He had been adopted as a child by a millionaire couple who didn't have any children of their own. They owned a lot of valuable real estate, and when his father died he intimidated and abused his mother until she signed everything over to him. He sold most of the property and spent the money on fast cars, drugs and prostitutes. He liked to throw hundreds of dollars from the second floor of the mall down to the lower floor just so he could watch people fight over it. He was abusive to everyone, especially women. I loved to fight for the thrill of it, but he wasn't like me—he was hateful and cruel to the core. I don't think he had any morals; he got his thrills out of watching others suffer. He would buy drugs for prostitutes to get them high and then physically abuse them, usually by biting, leaving awful, degrading scars on their bodies.

I was in the pool hall one day when he came in and started playing an arcade game, but he wasn't doing too well, and started shaking the machine. When he asked the kid behind the counter for more quarters and the kid refused to give him any, he grabbed and dragged him over the counter. I ran over, jumped up and kicked him in the head. He fell over and before he could get back up I jumped on him and beat him in the face until he was barely conscious. When I was done I dragged him outside and rolled him into a snow bank.

The kid behind the counter was a tall, slim kid named Scottie. We became good friends after that, and we are still good friends today. There's nothing I wouldn't do for Scottie, and I know he feels the same way about me.

A few weeks later the same big goof came back into the pool hall, the bruises on his face almost gone. He picked up a pool cue, smashed it across the first table he came to and said, "Langlais, I'm going to kill you!"

I went to the other side of the table and said, "Okay, but if we're going to fight, let's make it for money this time. How about we each put $500 on the table and the first one to go down loses?"

He agreed, so we each gave our money to Scottie and went out the back doors, and 40 or 50 people came along to watch. I imagine a few wagers were made, but most just came for the entertainment—they knew this was going to be good.

I looked up and said to him, "Remember the last time when I broke your face? Well, this time I'm going to take your f__ing head right off." I made a quick move for his head, and when he put his arms up to defend himself I swung my leg around and kicked the back of his knees out from under him, sending him falling over flat on his back. I turned around and went in to collect my money. We had agreed that the first one down was the loser, and he had gone down.

He came in the doors right behind me as mad as I have ever see anyone. We went at it, and I beat him so badly that an ambulance had to come. They picked him up from the sidewalk out front where I left him.

We kept seeing each other around town over the next year. He liked to gamble and had a lot of money to lose, so we crossed paths a few times. There was a quiet but uncomfortable truce between us. On Christmas Eve, as we were talking to each other in a nightclub just before closing, I asked him what he was doing for Christmas. "Nothing," he said. "What about you?" I wasn't doing anything either, so we decided that since the pool hall would be closed the next day we should go over to my place and play crib. We agreed to play for $100 a game.

We started playing on Christmas morning, and played for 17 hours straight. We didn't dare take our eyes off each other, even for a moment—the tension was unbelievable. We were both cheating, and we knew it. We had set the table up in the doorway between the kitchen and living room so that we were sitting at the table together but in different rooms. When a game was finished, whoever won threw the money on the floor behind him without looking away. We played, drank and smoked the entire day and on through the night. By the time he left the next morning, I had won almost two grand off him.

The third and last time we fought was a couple of months later while we were playing pool. There were two pool tables in the bar, so four of us were playing together. A buddy of mine ran the table on him and he got mad and backhanded him across the face. There was a fire extinguisher on the wall right behind me, so I grabbed it and yelled at him. He looked at me and came running. We met halfway across the room, and as we came together I drove the bottom of the fire extinguisher into his forehead so hard that his feet flew up in the air and he hit the ground, out cold. The rim at bottom of the tank actually dented his skull and left a permanent horseshoe-shaped mark just above his left eye.

He left town shortly after that for Vancouver where his violence and abuse of women continued to escalate. The last I heard he was doing a well-deserved life sentence for the role he played in the brutal murder of numerous young ladies in the Vancouver area.

Along with the violence and ugliness there were also times when my friends and I just had some plain old fun. One of our friends, Mike, was going through some hard times because his wife just divorced him and he had moved back into his parents' basement. We knew he was depressed, so we decided to cheer him up. He was out with us one evening, and after he went home a few of us went around town stealing every gnome we could find from people's yards (I was amazed at how many people had gnomes). We filled up my Bronco and the back of another truck, and then went back for more, ending up with probably over a hundred elves, leprechauns, animals, dwarfs and most of the Disney crew. We spent the next couple of hours at Mike's parent's house, carefully setting them up in what might be described as an "adult-rated" lawn sculpture.

The next morning Mike's dad wasn't exactly impressed with our creativity, and yelled at Mike to clean it up. He piled the gnomes up in the middle of the front yard, and later that day the local radio station announced that if your gnomes were missing they knew where you could find them. For the next three days people were driving up and searching through the pile for their gnomes.

I knew the police were watching me, so I was always on my guard. One day a guy started hanging around the pool hall, and I figured out pretty quickly that he was a narc. He had a lot of money, and seemed just a little too eager to part with it. He was hanging around, trying really hard to get into our circle, so I talked it over with my buddies and we decided we should let him in so that we could stay on top of what he was doing. For the next couple of months we let him think he was playing us, but we were actually playing him.

He was getting quite a bit of information from us, but I wasn't too worried because we weren't giving him anything really incriminating. If they wanted to make something stick they would need to nail us in a substantial drug deal. But he continued to put the pieces together, and after about three months we knew they were getting close to making their move, so we let him in on a big deal that was going down for Sunday at 11:00 a.m., behind the pool hall. That's the time the pool hall opened, so we explained to him that it was the best time to make the deal because, with a crowd of people standing around, nothing would look suspicious. Then I went for a walk with my buddies and told them to minus two. That meant we would back the whole thing up by two hours.

At 9:00 a.m. the deal went off without a hitch, without a cop in sight. About an hour later the police started setting up for their sting, plainclothes cops everywhere. When 11:00 a.m. came, we just went inside and started playing pool.

About a week later the police picked me up and brought me down to the station. They had spent months setting up that sting, and weren't too happy about what had happened. They pushed me hard, and started laying out all the information they had on me. After a while the undercover cop who had infiltrated our circle came into the interrogation room—I think he expected me to be surprised when I saw he was a cop. He tried to keep his cool, but I could see he was pretty embarrassed when I explained how we had been playing him the whole time.

The cop who was interrogating me wanted me to roll over and give up some of the bigger people above me, but I thought, "There's no way I'm going to be a big, fat, stinking rat." He had a lot of incriminating stuff on me, and said I had better play ball or he was going to come down hard on me. I listened as he told me all about my friends, my routines, and all the places I liked to go to. I was actually quite impressed with how much he knew about me.

As I sat there listening to him tell me everything about my life it began to dawn on me that two could play that game. He kept pushing me for information on the people above me, so I finally said, "Let me go and I'll call you in half an hour with my answer." He gave me his phone number and agreed to let me go for 30 minutes. I think he really expected me to roll.

When I left the police station I went straight to the pool hall and started asking questions about the cop who was interrogating me. It turned out that one of the guys working at the pool hall lived just a few houses down from him, and knew all about his family. In a few minutes I had all the information I needed. I used the phone right there to call back to the police station.

"It's pretty cool how you know all that stuff about me," I said. "Now let me tell you what I know about you." I then proceeded to tell him where he lived, his wife's name, the names of his two children and where they went to school and daycare, where his wife worked and what her shifts were. Then I hung up. I never threatened him in any way—I just told him what I knew. I waited for a while for the police to come and pick me up, but no one ever showed. I never heard from that cop again.

We had a good sized grow-op at a house that one of my friends was renting. There were several of us sleeping there one night when suddenly there were sirens and flashing lights all over the place. Our first thought was that they were coming for us, but when we looked out the window we saw that the house at the end of the block was on fire. We relaxed for a few minutes, but then saw that the police were going around to all the houses, getting people to evacuate. We also saw them checking out one of our cars parked out front. It just happened to be a car we had recently borrowed from a local dealership and hadn't gotten around to returning yet.

I didn't think it would be a good idea for the police to come to the door, and we could also see that they had discovered that the car was stolen. I looked the situation over and then came up with a plan. Most of the attention on the street was still being focused on the fire, but the police were definitely staking out the car as well. So I told the guys that I would walk out to the car and then reach into my pockets and make it look like I forgot the keys. Then I'd run back into the house. In that amount of time I would see how many cops were watching and exactly where they were. Then I would quickly run back out, jump into the car and lead them on a chase for as long as I could, maybe the next half hour or so. "That should give you guys enough time to get all this stuff cleaned out of here," I said. They agreed it was worth a shot.

It worked just the way we drew it up. While the police were chasing me around town for the next 30 minutes, the guys piled all the drugs and paraphernalia into a couple of trucks and moved it across town to a different house. I eventually got cornered and arrested, but it didn't take long for my buddies to come and bail me out of jail.

I was in Lethbridge for nearly six years. I continued to operate out of the nightclub and pool hall the whole time I was there. My life was filled with fighting, violence, sex, drugs and alcohol. But at the same time there was a growing emptiness that was beginning to gnaw at my guts. It was an emptiness that wouldn't go away and that I couldn't ignore.

CHAPTER 10

In the pool hall I used to hustle a couple of guys who always had lots of money. Just about everyone in Lethbridge had money, but it seemed to me that these particular two guys, Peter and Mike, had more money than they knew what to do with. They liked to party, and were definitely living the high life. I got to know them since they hung around the nightclub and pool hall where I was working, and found out they were vinyl siding salesmen. They told me that the money they were making on commissions was ridiculous, but that was obvious to me. They would reserve the table in the middle of the nightclub, order three or four bottles of the most expensive wine on the menu, dance, hit on the girls, do drugs and flaunt their money.

As we got to know each other better, they really seemed to take a liking to me. I looked after them and watched their backs, and they were good to me in return. I had a girlfriend at the time, and one day they told me they had made reservations for us at the nicest upscale restaurant and hotel in town. We were to order the most expensive thing on the menu, and it would be taken care of. I was a little nervous about this, but after the meal the waiter simply laid a room key on the table and told us to have a nice evening. He refused to take a tip, and insisted that everything had been more than adequately looked after.

The next time I saw Peter and Mike I told them I wanted to do what they were doing. The life they were living looked amazing to me, and I wanted in. They told me I would need to take a three-month training course to sell for the same company. I signed up the following week.

When I finished the course I went out on the road with them, and within a couple of days I knew I had hit the jackpot. It was the easiest money I had ever made. I was working under Peter and Mike, so they were taking a cut from my commission, but even then I was still sometimes pocketing over $1,000 on a single sale. Over the next few months I became a specialist at parting people from their money. I was a smooth talker, and it didn't take me long to learn how to pad my commission, write up unnecessary jobs and charge for work that was never even done.

One day they were bragging and having a good laugh about how they had written up a huge contract for two rich old ladies who lived just outside of town. I told them I could do better than they had done, so they wished me luck and told me to go for it. I took their signed contract with me and went back to the house where the ladies lived. I could see right away that Peter and Mike had been incredibly thorough, and there really wasn't anything more I could sell to these ladies. But I decided to see what I could do anyway.

I spent the next hour basically apologizing for wasting their time. I told them I had actually been planning to rip them off by getting them to sign a contract for renovations they obviously didn't need, but I had a change of heart because I could see they were such nice people. I went on, making up a story about how I desperately needed $5,000 to pay off a debt, quickly adding that I would try to make a sale somewhere else. I sold my story so well that they ended up just giving me the $5,000 in 100-dollar bills.

I found Peter and Mike in back the pool hall. I walked up to them and said, "You guys did a great job. There was nothing left for me to sell those old birds." They started to smile at each other, and then I pulled out the wad of 100-dollar bills from my pocket. "So I sold them myself," I said, and threw the money up in the air. They couldn't believe it, but they had to admit that I was good, and we had a great laugh about it.

I kept working under them for the next year, and then decided I had learned enough to go out on my own. I knew that if I was making $1,000 or more on a sale even with them taking their cut, then they must be making a lot more than that. They weren't overly pleased with my decision, but there really wasn't anything they could do about it. We remained friends, and sometimes we even had friendly competitions to see who could make the biggest sale or pull off the biggest scam.

By now I had moved out of the basement of the sub shop and was living in a nice condo. Along with selling siding I was still taking care of things down at the sub shop, bouncing at the nightclub and solving problems for other people whenever I was called on. I also became good buddies with my roommate Byron, a bouncer at a local biker bar called the Alex Arms Hotel. We partied together and did lots of drugs. I was bringing in thousands of dollars every week, and more money just meant more drugs.

The Alex Arms Hotel opened a couple hours earlier than the club, so one evening I went to see Byron and maybe have a drink or two before I went to work. There was a pretty young lady sitting at a table by herself, so naturally I went over to join her. I had seen her around my nightclub a couple of times, and thought this might be a good opportunity to introduce myself. I had just taken a seat and started talking to her when a big biker came over and told me quite explicitly that it would be in my best interest to leave, the sooner the better. I took a sip of my drink and looked up at him. The first thing I noticed was his bright red hair. The second thing I noticed was that he was huge, with arms like telephone poles!

I leaned over to the girl and asked her if she knew this guy, and she said no.

Again, he insisted I leave, and added a few expletives to make sure I got the point.

I asked him if he was referring to me, and said this was no way to be talking in front of a lady. As we exchanged a few more pleasantries I slowly adjusted my position, sitting up straight and crossing my right leg over the top of my left one. That way my leg was ready to kick the moment he made a move for me—kind of the way a rattlesnake coils back, ready to strike.

He suddenly made a grab for me, and my foot shot up into his face. I grabbed his bright red hair, smashing his head down hard into my knee. I pulled his head up again and smashed it into the edge of the table. That was all I had time for, because five or six other bikers were already rushing at me. I had hurt him badly and he was like a giant rag doll in my hands, so I threw him into the path of the oncoming bikers and headed for the exit. I loved to fight, but I also knew when it was time to get out.

I didn't think anything more about Big Red until the first week I was out selling siding on my own. It had been a few months since the fight, but I guess Big Red remembered me. I was standing on the front porch of a house, having just introduced myself to a nice senior lady, and was beginning my sales pitch. Suddenly, I heard tires screeching to a stop on the road behind me. I turned around and saw Big Red get out of a bright yellow 1974 Nova, and come towards us with a crowbar in his hand. "You!" he yelled, pointing at me.

"Excuse me for a moment, ma'am," I said. "Maybe you should call 9-1-1." Then I headed out to meet Big Red on the road.

We fought out there on the street for a couple of minutes. I was going backwards because he was a big boy and he was swinging that crowbar like he meant business. I kept deflecting it off to the side, and each time the crowbar went past my face I quickly got in a shot to his head. During the course of the fight I broke both of my hands—one when he hit me with the crowbar, and one when I punched him on the top of his head. He had a tough skull.

I was slowly going backwards down the road, and out of the corner of my eye I saw we were getting close to a parked car. As soon as I felt the car against my legs I grabbed him by the shirt, threw myself sideways and used his own momentum to drive his face hard into the bumper. That turned things in my favour. I squeezed his head between my broken hands and started smashing his face against the hood and grill.

The lady must have called 9-1-1 like I asked her, because I could now hear the sirens. Suddenly a couple of police cars, a fire truck and ambulance were all on the scene. One of the policemen ran over and yelled, "Langlais, what are you doing?"

"He's trying to kill me with a crowbar!" I said.

Big Red was already in bad shape and I wasn't slowing down, so the policeman drew his gun and said, "Stop!" I looked up and saw that, along with the one gun that was already pointed at me, the other police all had their hands on their guns, too.

"Not until you take his crowbar away," I said, as I smashed Big Red's head one more time.

He was pretty much unconscious and probably didn't have the capacity to let go of the crowbar, so the policeman reached over and took it out of his hand.

"There," I said, "that's all I wanted." I let him fall onto the hood of the car, and the ambulance guys came over and rolled him onto the stretcher. It was going to take a bit of work to put his face back together.

When the police looked over the scene and talked to the lady at the house, they decided I had acted in self-defense. I couldn't fill out the incident report because of my broken hands, so they filled it out for me. They asked me if I wanted to press charges, but I thought Big Red had probably learned his lesson, and they agreed.

A week later, with one hand in a cast, I was back selling siding. One of the first sales I made was for a $13,500 job. That was a big sale, and I felt pretty good about the $1,000 commission I had worked in for myself. When I brought it back to my boss, Cam, who owned the siding company, he just shook his head. "Let me show you how this is done," he said.

He was smooth. He took me back to the house where I had made the sale and started off by apologizing to the homeowner for what I had done. He explained that I was new and didn't really know what I was doing. I watched in amazement as he went through the whole contract, reworking the numbers, changing a few of the jobs that we would be doing, cancelling a few others altogether. The final contract was still for exactly the same amount, but my commission had tripled!

"That's the way you make a sale," he said to me as we drove away.

That opened up a whole new world to me. I learned how to spin a contract so I could make as much commission as I wanted. I learned how to bring a partner with me and then "fire" him while we were sitting in the homeowner's living room putting the finishing touches on a contract. I'd send him out to the car, and then tell the homeowners how sorry and embarrassed I was about how the new guy had written up such a poor work order. Then I'd rework the whole thing, with them thinking they were getting a much better deal. Legally you were only allowed to make a 40% commission, but on some of the contracts I got 200 or 300%! It sometimes took some fancy paperwork to cover up what I was doing, and though I wasn't very good at paperwork there was money to be made, so I did what I needed to do.

After I learned the trade a little bit better I started making road trips. Saskatchewan had just brought in a government grant program for home renovations, and the money was there for the taking. I signed on as a sales rep with three different companies and headed for Regina. No matter what kind of home improvements someone was looking for, I could write up a contract for anything. Siding, windows, doors, any kind of upgrade—I sold them all.

The amount of money I made was crazy! I was a smooth talker, but that was only part of it. There was a lot of grant money available, and people were scrambling to get their hands on it. Usually it didn't take much of a sales pitch before someone would sign on the dotted line.

One day I wrote up a contract for an elderly Ukrainian couple. They were arguing back and forth with each other about everything, which I found quite entertaining. At first they just wanted some basement work done, so I wrote up a contract for $2,400 worth of work. Of that total, my commission was going to be around $700, but after the contract was drawn up they started asking about windows and a few other things for the upstairs part of the house. I reworked the numbers and ended up with a work order for $3,400, with my take being $1,000, which I thought that was all right. The wife had gone into the kitchen at this point, working on dinner, and when she heard what the total was going to be, she yelled out, "Is that for everything?"

I was about to say, "Yes, that's the total amount," but before I could say anything the husband cut me off.

"No, are you stupid?" he yelled back at her. "That's just for the basement. If we want all the rest of it done it's another $3,400."

"That's right," I said.

They wrote me a cheque for the first $3,400 right there, and agreed to pay the other half when the work was done. When I showed the cheque to my boss, he shook his head in disbelief. All that money went straight into my pocket and I still made $1,000 commission besides.

As fast as I was making money though, I was spending it on drugs. My coke habit began to control more and more of my life to the point where I couldn't go more than an hour or two without a fix. I'd do a line of coke in my car before I went up to a house for a sales call, and then I'd do another one as soon as I got back. Sometimes I wouldn't leave my motel room for a few days at a time. I would just sit there the whole time drinking and doing drugs. Then I'd go out and make enough sales in one day to keep me going for another week.

On the weekends I was still going back to Lethbridge to party at the pool hall and nightclubs. My friends were starting to tell me my life was way out of control, and though I knew it too I didn't know how to stop what I was doing. I felt trapped in a cycle of addictions, getting in deeper and deeper all the time, but I had to keep going. I couldn't stop.

There were times when I needed to hire someone to drive me around because I was too stoned to drive anywhere myself. I hated what I was doing, and started to hate myself. I knew that some of the people I was ripping off couldn't afford what I was charging them, but I needed their money. My addictions were costing me thousands of dollars a week.

It was the ugliest time in my life. Along with the coke I was doing, I was drinking crazy amounts of Kahlua every day, but still I could never get enough. There was a constant craving for more. Trying to say no to that craving would have been like trying to not go to the bathroom when I really had to go. My mind could think of nothing else except putting more and more drugs into my system.

And so entered crack. Crack is pure, concentrated cocaine with all of the additives and impurities burned off. I started going on crack binges whenever I could. For this I needed a test tube, ammonia, a box of penny matches, a couple of cartons of cigarettes, a razor blade, a few bags of ice and some candles. I found that the camping candles you find at Esso stations worked well because they burn slowly, and come in packages of five.

I would arrange everything on the table in front of me, and then light a candle and about half a dozen cigarettes. I'd let the cigarettes burn slowly in an ashtray to get a good supply of ashes. About a gram of cocaine was put into the test tube first, and then the ammonia was carefully poured in—you needed to be careful because it was a volatile combination. The right mixture was four parts ammonia to one part cocaine. The test tube was then held over the burning candle and shaken for just a few seconds. That's all it took for the powder to turn into a purified rock floating in the liquid.

Usually I would try to build up a small pile of rocks before I started smoking it, but sometimes I couldn't wait that long. To smoke it I would shave off some flakes with a razor blade, pack some of the cigarette ashes into my pipe, put a few flakes on top of the ashes and ignite it with a match. Then I'd add a few more flakes and inhale. It was instant euphoria.

Within 60 to 90 seconds I was lusting for another hit—that's why I needed the ice. There was no time for my pipe to cool down on its own between hits. If I didn't put it on ice, then it would get too hot to hold after a while.

While I was smoking crack I was constantly checking my pulse. I had heard that if your heart rate got above 200 beats per minute you would die, so I tried to keep my pulse at around 180. I would hold my wrist for 30 seconds and count the beats. As long as it was around 90 I knew I was okay. If I had enough cocaine to keep going I would sometimes sit at a table for two days straight, or even longer. I wouldn't sleep, eat or drink. I would just do drugs, and go to the bathroom when I had to. I would force myself to drink something once in a while so I wouldn't get dehydrated. It was normal to lose a few pounds in body weight by the time I was done.

Sometimes I was alone on these binges, but usually there would be several of us who would get together at a motel room somewhere. One of the side effects of crack is extreme paranoia, so we would hire someone to be in the room with us, and watch the windows to make sure no one was coming.

Whenever we started out as a group it always ended with me by myself. As the supply went down the tension would rise, and I would say, "There's not much left, boys. We're getting down to the end, boys." They would take the hint, and one by one they would leave. They wanted it just as badly as I did, but I would have thrown them through the walls for those last few flakes, and they knew it.

Coming down after the drugs were gone was a totally desperate, empty, shallow, rage-filled experience. I would literally be on my hands and knees searching underneath the couch cushions and between the fibres of the carpet for any flakes that might have dropped to the floor. Every part of my body was screaming for more. I would have killed someone for just one more hit. After searching every nook and cranny I would crawl over to the bed and lie there for five or six hours, trying to pass out and get some sleep, but my body would be so wound up that sleep wouldn't come.

There are days and even weeks of time from this period of my life that I have absolutely no recollection of. There were times when I woke up in a motel room having no idea where I was, how long I had been there or even how I got there. I sometimes had to go outside and look around for a while before I could even figure out what town I was in, or I'd have to call the front desk to ask when I had checked in and where I was.

I was putting more drugs into my body all the time. I knew I was heading for a train wreck, but I didn't feel like I could do anything about it, and wasn't even sure I wanted to do anything about it. I was pushing myself to the edge, and was hovering on the thin line between life and death.

Somehow, through this whole time, I kept making sales. I can't believe people signed the contracts, because there were days when I could barely sign my own name, let alone fill out a work order. Some of the contracts I wrote up didn't make any sense, and the office would have to send someone after me to redo the measurements. They charged me $50 every time they had to rewrite one of my contracts, which was becoming more frequent.

And through all of this I was still a finely-tuned fighting machine. I kept up my regular workout routines, and made sure that my conditioning, reflexes and senses were in top shape. I needed to be able to instantly turn on that switch whenever the situation called for it.

I kept my eyes and ears open for what I liked to call "grapes." A grape was an opportunity ripe for the picking. One day, while I was sitting in a Lethbridge casino playing the slots, someone asked for my help. He said he had just been ripped off five lbs. of pot. He explained that he owed these guys some money and that he was planning on paying them back as soon as he sold the drugs. They knew this, but they had gotten impatient and stolen it from him. I knew the individuals involved, and what they had done didn't seem quite fair to me.

I asked him what my cut would be. "I'll give you one pound," he said.

I figured that would be worth about $2,500. "Watch my things," I told him. "I'll be right back."

I went over to their apartment and kicked in the door. There were three or four guys sitting there with a few guns and knives lying around, but fortunately nobody was foolish enough to make a move for anything. I told them what I thought of their actions, and after I explained their options to them, they agreed they had made an error in judgment, and it would be best for everyone involved if this was settled peacefully. They handed over the stuff, and five minutes later I was back in my seat at the casino.

That was a grape. There were always grapes, ready to be picked.

One of the other salesmen I got to know was Eddie, a big, black, round guy who kind of reminded me of a black Santa Claus. He was from the Detroit area, but knew there was good money to be made in Saskatchewan, and since he considered himself a bit of a high roller he had come up for a while to get in on the action. He was 20 years older than me, drove a big white Cadillac, and loved to party. He was into the drugs and booze too, but when he saw how I was living, he started to get concerned about me.

One day when we met up in Saskatoon, he asked if I wanted to take a trip with him to a town in northern Saskatchewan, to make a few sales together. But more than that, he thought I should just take it easy for a while, and that maybe a change of scenery would do me some good. On the drive up we talked about how I needed to take some time to just lay low and get my life back on track.

When we got into town we pulled up to the first hotel we saw. Inside, the front desk was to the right and the bar was to the left. "You check us in, and I'll see you in there," I said, pointing to the left.

When Eddie joined me a few minutes later a bit of a situation had developed. He shook his head and looked at me as if to say, "Already? Couldn't you even stay out of trouble for a couple of minutes?"

He turned to go and said, "I'll go start the car." He'd already seen me in a few fights, and knew I could handle whatever I had gotten myself into, so he didn't feel the need to stay. Besides, he knew it would probably be best if we could make a quick exit after whatever was about to happen was over.

As it happened, I had just taken a seat at the bar and ordered a drink when a guy came over, informing me that I would be buying him and his four friends the next round of refreshments. They had seen me pull out my wad of cash and knew it wouldn't be a problem for me to pay for their drinks. I let him know that buying anyone a drink wasn't in my plans, and that he probably shouldn't ask again. He went back and told his friends what I had said, and they all got up and came over. They told me that if I knew what was good for me I would be buying them their drinks for the rest of the evening.

"Are you guys frikin' retarded?" I asked. "Didn't you understand what I told this goof here?" Then, just to make sure that there was no further misunderstanding, I added a few other suggestions of where they could take themselves and their ideas and what they could do when they got there.

They still didn't get it. They told me that if I didn't buy them a drink they were going to beat me up and take my money.

I couldn't believe this was actually happening. "Would you guys like to step outside to solve this problem there?" I asked.

They seemed quite eager to do that, so I headed for the door and they followed. As soon as I stepped through the doorway out onto the landing I spun around and grabbed the first guy. It just took a second to snap a few of his bones. The other guys were still coming out the door behind him, and before they realized what was happening I pushed the first guy back into the second guy and knocked him off balance. I hit the second guy so hard that I knocked him unconscious and sent him headfirst down the concrete steps. He was probably 240 lbs., and he landed hard on his head. Then I grabbed the third guy by the throat and threw him off to the side. I reached for the last two guys, but they were already running in the other direction.

The fight, if you could call it that, was over in a few seconds. Eddie was already there with the door of his Cadillac swung open. "Let's go! Let's go!" he was yelling. To get to his car I had to jump over the guy who had fallen down the steps. I quickly glanced down at him, seeing a pool of blood starting to form around his head, and I knew instantly he was in serious trouble. I jumped in and we peeled out of there.

The drive back to Saskatoon was stressful, to say the least. I was wound up so tight that we had to stop every half hour just so I could walk around and smoke a joint to try to calm myself down. At one point we saw a bunch of police lights flashing on the road ahead of us. We weren't sure if it was a road block or if anyone was even looking for us, but we weren't going to take that chance. So, we turned off and drove along some back roads for a while.

After driving all night, Eddie dropped me off in Saskatoon in the morning. He said he didn't need any trouble at this point in his life, so he was heading back home to Detroit. So I called up Bill, another salesman I knew, who said I could stay with him for a while at his apartment. We had spent time before selling siding and dealing drugs together, so I figured we could pick up where we had left off. But before long he saw that my drug habit was way out of control and I had gotten too crazy for him. He moved out almost immediately after I moved in.

I was very aware that I was hitting another low point in my life, lower than I had ever been before. I was alone, I was destroying my body with drugs and alcohol and I was getting sick of hurting people. I started to feel an overwhelming emptiness inside, and at some point during the next few days

I came to the decision that I would just kill myself. I couldn't think of a single reason to go on living. I took stock of what drugs and booze I had left and figured I had enough to last me about four more days. I didn't want it to go to waste, so I picked up a bottle of Kahlua and sat out on the second storey balcony overlooking the parking lot. "Four days," I thought, "and then I'll put a bullet in my head."

I sat out on that balcony for most of the next four days. I went inside a few times to sleep on the couch for a couple of hours and do some crack, but mostly I spent the time just sitting on the balcony drinking, twirling a gun around on my finger and waiting for the time to arrive when I would end my life.

It was Friday night, and a bunch of cars filled with teenagers started showing up in the parking lot. I hadn't noticed before, but now I realized there was a church across the lot facing my balcony. There was some sort of a youth gathering going on, and soon the place was filled with kids making a bunch of noise and running all over the place. They partied until late that night before they finally left. I was glad when they were gone, because the sight of all those young people laughing and having a good time was making me mad.

The next morning the parking lot started to fill up again. This time it was a wedding, and again that entire day people kept coming and going. They were smiling and laughing, and again it made me mad. I thought, "How can they be so happy while I'm sitting here in such a rage?" What right did they have to be having such a good time?

The next morning I couldn't believe it—the parking lot started to fill up with cars again! It seemed like hundreds of cars just kept coming, and the people were all going into the church for another party, I assumed, though I had no idea what went on in there. I'd been to plenty of nightclubs, so it seemed to me that with that many people showing up, there had to be one heck of a party going on.

While I sat on the balcony watching people coming and going, I kept getting angrier and more depressed all the time. Even the shining sun made me angry. Why did it have to be a nice day? Why couldn't it be gloomy and grey like I was feeling? My drugs were running out, so I could see the end was coming, which made me happy but also scared me. I wasn't sure I actually wanted to die, but I had no reason to live. I just knew I had to find some way out of the personal hell that my life had turned into, and couldn't see any other way.

My only concern was Rena—I didn't know how she would respond. I remembered how Dean had called me just before he had blown his head off, and I wondered if I should call Rena and let her know what I was going to do. In the end I decided I wouldn't. I tried to lie down on the couch to get some sleep, but whenever I closed my eyes awful images and memories came flooding back.

Around noon the cars in the parking lot started to leave and I thought that now, finally, I would get some peace and quiet. But at 6:00 p.m. they all came back again. I couldn't believe how hard these people partied and how happy they all seemed to be! Their happiness was literally making me sick to my stomach. They partied for a couple of hours that evening and then went back home again.

On Monday the place was dead quiet. I couldn't figure out what was going on. These people partied all weekend and then nobody showed up for work on Monday! It blew me away. The only thing I knew for sure was that I wouldn't be around to see them partying again next weekend.

I sat out there all day on the balcony, and with nothing to see or think about my mind started to race back and forth through the sights and sounds of my life. Voices and images from my past started playing like a recording in my head. "I wish you had never been born. I wish you were dead. I should have killed you. You're a freak. You're retarded. You're a dog!" Faces that I'd bloodied and beaten, and bodies that I'd left lying broken in the streets and back alleys all flashed through my mind. All day long the ugliness played over and over in my head—I couldn't shut it off.

That night the crack ran out. All I had left was a little bit of pot and a few bottles of booze, but that was okay with me. Tomorrow, when my last bottle was empty, I would put a revolver to my head and put an end to all this pain and ugliness that I was living in—this hell I had created.

Early next morning a big green car pulled into the parking lot. I figured it was the janitor coming to clean up the mess from the weekend. I'd been to enough parties to know what the inside of that place must look like, and I felt kind of sorry for him when I thought about the job he had ahead of him.

He got out of his car and started walking towards the church doors. I was still curious about everything that had gone on there over the weekend, so I stood up and yelled to him, "Hey you! Come here!"

He looked in my direction and then around the parking lot to see who I was yelling at. Then he looked back at me, pointing to his chest as if to ask, "Are you talking to me?"

"Yeah, you!" I shouted. "Come here!"

He walked up to the chain link fence that separated the parking lot from my apartment building and looked up at me. "Those guys partied hard all weekend," I said. "You've got quite a mess to clean up." He didn't seem to quite understand what I was getting at.

"What are you doing?" he asked.

"I'm just finishing off all this junk," I said, holding up my bottle. "Then I'm going to take myself out of the picture. Today should be my last day."

He looked at me and didn't seem quite sure what he should do or say next. "Can I come up there and talk to you for a minute?" he asked.

"Sure," I said. "Come on up." I told him what room, and then buzzed him in.

He walked into my living room and stood there looking around. The place must have smelled pretty bad from all the dope I'd been doing. There were empty bottles lined up on the coffee table and drug paraphernalia all over the place. A few throwing stars and knives were lying around, and my gun was there on a chair. He looked the place over and then motioned towards the church and said, "Why don't we go over there and talk?"

I lifted my bottle. "As long as I can bring this along."

He nodded.

I smoked a joint as we walked across the parking lot. I still thought he was the janitor, and I was looking forward to seeing the mess he had to clean up. He unlocked the door and I followed him as he led the way down a hall. He stopped in front of a door marked "Pastor."

"Hey," I said, "you're not the janitor."

"No," he said, "I'm the pastor. My name is Ralph." He opened the door and we walked into his office. "What's your name?" he asked.

"Rick."

He sat down behind his desk and I sat across from him. I could see he was nervous, but his spirit was so gentle, and I started to feel something strange stirring inside of me.

"Why would you want to kill yourself?" he asked.

"I'm not a good person," I answered.

"Jesus loves you," he said.

"Nobody loves me, pal," I shot back.

"Jesus loves you," he said again.

"No, you don't understand," I argued. "I've done a lot of bad things. I sell drugs. I hurt people. My own mother hated me. No one loves me."

"Jesus does," he said.

"I've destroyed people," I went on. "I've quashed people. I hurt people for money. I'm a bad person!"

"There's a story in the Bible about a man who hurt a lot of people," he said. "His name is Paul, and he hurt people and killed people. But God turned his life around."

Ralph kept trying to convince me that God loved me, and that it didn't have to end like this, and I kept repeating that no one loved me. No one could possibly love someone like me!

"What do you have to lose by giving Jesus a try?" he finally asked. "He might change your life. He might give you a reason for living."

I could feel tears starting to well up in my eyes. I had never been a coward, and I had never backed down or bowed down to anyone, but now I could feel myself breaking. Something strange was happening inside of me. Pastor Ralph again said something about God changing me and giving me a new life, and giving me a reason for living, if I would just give Him a chance.

His words played over in my mind. A reason for living—that's what I needed.

"How would I know?" I asked. "How would I do that?"

He reached over and picked up a little yellow pamphlet from the shelf beside his desk and opened it up.

I felt the anger starting to rise again. He just wasn't getting it! Nobody loved me! His Jesus wasn't going to make any difference! I was vibrating with anger.

I stood up and grabbed the pamphlet out of his hand and opened it up. I tried to read it, but my hands were shaking and there were tears in my eyes. I couldn't focus on the words. Suddenly, I felt myself dropping to my knees. I knelt there on the floor shaking. The tears started streaming down my face.

Pastor Ralph came around his desk and knelt beside me. He asked if I would like him to read the booklet to me. He then took it from my hands and started to read some words about God loving me and sending His Son to die for me. He read that God wanted to forgive me, to come into my life and have a relationship with me. There was a prayer at the end of the booklet, and he asked if I wanted to say it after him.

He read the prayer, and I heard myself repeating it line for line as he read:

Dear Lord Jesus
I know that I am a sinner who needs your forgiveness
I believe that you died for my sins
I want to turn from my sins
I now invite you to come into my life
I want to trust and follow you

After we finished the prayer I got up off my knees, and I felt so light and free. It literally felt like something had been flushed from my body. I felt like suddenly I was okay, and that maybe things really could be different. I wanted to change, and in that moment I felt that there might actually be a chance. I had hope. There was no doubt in my mind that something powerful—something real—had just happened to me.

The first words out of my mouth were, "I've got some friends that need to hear about this."

CHAPTER 11

Pastor Ralph and I talked for a few more minutes, but I don't remember much of what was said, except that he said he would come over to my place later in the day. I walked back across the parking lot to my apartment still feeling strangely wonderful and light. It was a different kind of high than I had ever felt before. The drugs just masked the pain and made me feel good on the outside, but this feeling was coming from somewhere deep inside me.

When I got to my apartment I cleaned myself up and then started to tidy up the place as best as I could. The place was a disaster, so I started to put a few things away. For some reason it just seemed like the right thing to do. Pastor Ralph stopped in later that afternoon and told me he had talked to his wife, who was expecting me at their house for supper.

Supper that evening blew me away. Grace, Ralph's wife, was a tiny, sweet lady, who smiled and welcomed me with a warmth like I couldn't remember ever seeing before. They had two children, an 11-year-old boy named Linden, and a 9-year-old girl named Luanne. There was a peace and gentleness in their home that evening that I couldn't comprehend. I remember thinking that it didn't seem right—people just didn't treat each other like that.

When I was introduced to Linden I reached out and rubbed him on the top of his head. "Hey little buddy, how ya doin'?" I asked. He didn't say anything, but gave me a big smile, and we seemed to hit it off right away. I found out later that "Bud" was the nickname his dad had for him. The thought struck me that these kids looked like wholesome apple pie. They were just little, innocent, healthy kids, so pure and polite. They washed their hands before meals, bowed their heads to say grace, and spoke politely to each other. It was ridiculous!

After supper Luanne played a song on the piano. I thought she looked like an angel sitting there as she played. As I listened, the tears started to run down my face again. I didn't make any sound, but I felt the salt water burning my cheeks.

All that evening I was torn between thinking there was no way this was real—this had to be a show that they were putting on—and thinking that I might actually be on the road to this. One minute I was thinking about how long they must have rehearsed this "play," that I just couldn't accept that any of it was real, and they had to be faking it. But then the next minute I would break down and start to hope that maybe this kind of life was possible, maybe even for me.

Over the next few weeks Pastor Ralph and I continued to either get together or talk on the phone every day. I started going to church on Sunday mornings, and right away I began to see the same kind of warmth and love in the people there that I had seen in Pastor Ralph and his family. Some people in the church were uncomfortable around me and didn't know what to say, but for the most part they were just a bunch of friendly, caring people. I decided that either a lot of people were pretending, or this was actually real.

I didn't get a lot out of the sermons in those first few months, but the singing was amazing! It was powerful. When the music played and hundreds of people stood singing together something would stir inside of me. I wanted what these people had more than anything I had ever wanted before, but at the same time I knew I was very different from them. I was a hardcore drug addict and a fighter. I had an impossibly long road to travel if I was ever going to be like them, and I didn't know how I would ever get there.

I decided to take a couple of weeks off from selling siding to concentrate on pulling myself together. I told myself I would drink less and start kicking a few habits. I knew it wouldn't be easy, but I was determined to give it a try at least. What I didn't know was that the toughest battles of my life were ahead of me.

After church one day I was approached by two old ladies. They had heard there was a new Christian in church, so they came looking for me. Gertrude and Anne Huebert were sisters who had never married and had lived together their whole lives. They were warriors of a different kind than I had ever met before. They were prayer warriors, and they told me they were praying for me. I sensed that these two gentle, loving ladies were powerful warriors for God.

When they asked what kind of work I did, I explained that I was in the home renovation business. They said they had just moved into their new house and were thinking about getting a backyard fence put up. I tried not to smile as I asked if I could have a look at the project, but they told me they had already gotten a price from the contractor who had built the house just the year before.

"That's fantastic!" I said. "Why don't I come over, and we'll see if we're comparing apples to oranges?" A couple of days later, on a nice sunny morning, they showed me their big back yard, and I asked them what kind of a fence they wanted. They told me again that they had already received a proposal, but after I coaxed them a bit more, they invited me inside to have a look at the contract. At their kitchen table they handed me the paper showing a bid for $1,743.

I said, "Ladies, I can build that same fence for $3,400."

Gertrude, the feistier of the two, was eyeballing me. After a few seconds of silently staring at me she asked, "Why would it cost twice as much for you to build it?"

I could see she was a straight shooter, so I fired right back, "I'm a drug addict, and I've got expenses. But if you want that fence built to your satisfaction, I can do it."

They looked at each other, communicating in some way that I couldn't see, and then wrote me a cheque for half the job up front. When I finished the fence the next week they gave me the other $1,700.

Gertrude passed away a few years ago, but Anne, now in her 90s, still prays regularly for me and Hands On Ministry. She's one of the behind-the-scenes warriors that keeps the ministry going.

I was getting to know a few other people in the church, too. One couple invited me to their place a few times, and though it was obvious I was battling with all sorts of issues and addictions, that didn't seem to matter to them. They just loved me and welcomed me into their home. Their names were Ed and Mary Schroeder, but they told me I could call them Ma and Pa. I didn't know it then, but they would become two of the most important people in my life. One day I met them for

Ed & Mary Schroeder

breakfast at the Sandman Inn at 11:30 a.m., but we ended up sitting there all day talking, even having our supper there too, and not leaving until late that evening. I told them my story while they sat and listened. They didn't judge or criticize me in any way. They just loved me for who I was. I started spending more and more time at their place and they truly became like loving parents to me. There were a lot of tough struggles and some pretty dark times ahead, but they patiently stood by me no matter what.

I kept attending church every Sunday, and after a while I started bringing some of my friends with me. We'd be partying all Saturday night and then I'd tell them we were going to church together the next morning, because that's just what I did. None of them had any idea how to act in church, and sometimes we looked and smelled quite interesting after being up all night partying. Some of the church people kept their distance, but most of them accepted us and tried their best to make us feel welcome. Eventually some of my friends didn't want to go out with me anymore on Saturday nights because they knew it would mean going to church in the morning.

After the bars closed one Saturday night, a few of us went over to the church parking lot around 3:00 a.m. to throw a Frisbee around. We had been partying hard and were feeling pretty good, so we didn't want to call it a night just yet. We decided to just hang out there in the parking lot until church started. After a while the police showed up and asked us what we were doing. My friend Darwin (who was fairly inebriated) walked over to the policeman, pointed to the church and said, "We're going to that church in the morning." To explain more, he went on, "We're just trying to…" and that's as far as he got before he threw up all over the officer's shoes. The policeman stared down at his shoes for a few seconds, looked around at us and then shook his head. Without a word, he got back into his car and drove away.

I talked freely about my relationship with God to all my friends, and although I was trying to change my life it was obvious I wasn't making much progress. I was maybe drinking a little bit less and doing a few less drugs, but the progress was painfully slow. I wanted to change, but I didn't see how I could. Drugs, alcohol and violence were all I knew. I couldn't see any way out of the life I was living. Occasionally I would have a good day, and at least for a little while I would think that I might have a chance of changing. But those faint glimmers of hope were few and far between. It seemed that every time I took a step forward something would happen to knock me backward again. I was a hardcore addict, and inside I knew I was stuck in an endless cycle.

All this time I was still living in the apartment next to the church. I'd seen the landlord's daughter, in her late teens or early 20s, around the apartment complex a few times, and I knew she liked to party. She started coming up to my place to drink and smoke pot, and one night we ended up sleeping together. A few evenings later the landlord was at my door, not too happy. He told me to pack my stuff and get out. "The place isn't even registered in your name, so I'm evicting you," he said. "And," he added, "if you ever touch my daughter again, I will rip your frikin' head off!"

I was a little bit stunned. Nobody talked to me that way. Nobody ever threatened me and got away with it.

I looked at him and said, "Pardon me?"

"I'm an ex-Green Beret," he said, "and if you ever come near my daughter again, I will kill you."

"Really, you're an ex-Green Beret? Stop this!" I said, as I kicked him hard in the groin. As he doubled over, I hit him in the face with an upper cut, sending him sprawling backwards across the hall. I knew I had made solid contact because I could see the blood running out of his broken nose. I slammed the door and walked back into my apartment.

I was vibrating with anger and needed to talk to someone, so I called Ma Schroeder. We talked for about 10 minutes, and just as she was starting to calm me down someone pounded on my door. "I'll just take care of this, and then I'll be right back," I told her.

I put the phone down and started walking towards the door. As I reached for it I could hear someone trying to work a key into the lock, so I quickly pulled the door open and saw a huge gorilla of a man who seemed to fill the whole doorway. The landlord was standing behind him, peeking around his shoulder. "That's the guy," he said, pointing at me. "Throw him out."

I wasn't going to just stand there and wait for Johnny Gorilla to make the first move, so I hit him in the chest with my elbow hard enough that I felt his breastplate crack. He collapsed right there in my doorway, and as soon as he hit the floor I stepped over him and fed the landlord a few more punches. Then I kicked Johnny out of my doorway, and left them both lying there in the hallway.

I got back on the phone with Ma and told her what had happened. We talked for a while, and again as she was getting me calmed down there was another knock on the door. I couldn't believe they were coming back for more! These guys just didn't know when to quit. "Hang on, Ma," I said, "I'll be right back."

I felt it was going to get ugly. I wondered how many guys were on the other side of the door this time, but it really didn't matter. I was ready to use whatever force was needed to end this.

There were a few weapons lying around, so I picked one up and started towards the door. I wasn't sure what to expect the third time around, but I wasn't going to take any chances. Before I got to the door it swung open and in walked two police officers together with Johnny Gorilla and the landlord. The first person through the door was a female officer with her gun drawn. Her partner was right behind her with his hand on his gun, too. I stopped in my tracks.

The female officer did the talking. "Just calm down, Rick," she said. "Relax and put the weapon down."

I stood there for a few seconds looking the situation over, wondering what to do. We were at a standoff. They had toys; I had toys. Now what? I was looking the situation over, trying to calculate what it would take for me to get out of this one.

"I want you to back up slowly and look outside," she said, very calm and gentle.

Without taking my eyes off them I slowly backed up until I could feel the curtain to the sliding door. I pushed it aside, looked out through the glass, and counted seven police cars parked under my balcony and around the parking lot. Red and blue lights were flashing all over the place.

"We want you to come with us," she went on. "We're not charging you with anything right now. We just want to talk to you."

I carefully took a couple of steps back to the middle of the room where I had left the phone. Ma was still on the other end of the line. "I think I'm going to go with these guys," I said to her. "And Ma," I quickly added, "call Pastor Ralph." I hung up the phone, put my weapon down on the coffee table and turned around so they could handcuff me.

I spent the night in jail, and the next morning Pastor Ralph was there to pick me up. The police decided the landlord had been the instigator, and I was just defending myself. Pastor Ralph spoke up in my defense, and on his recommendation they let me go. They told me I wasn't allowed to go back to the apartment, so a couple of men from the church got my stuff and cleaned up the place as best they could. From there I moved into the Confederation Inn Motel for the next few months.

Bad things seemed to just keep coming at me. It wasn't that I was looking for trouble; I was honestly trying to keep to myself, but just like when I was in school I couldn't seem to avoid getting into fights. Trouble just showed up at my door, sometimes literally. One night I heard some commotion outside my door, so I stepped into the hall to see what was going on. Two guys had tried to get a room, but the front desk manager refused to give them one because they were obviously intoxicated and were being rather impolite and unruly. I asked the manager if he needed help, but he said the police had already been called, and everything was under control. That was good with me, so I turned to go back into my room.

The two guys smelled the drugs I was smoking though, and they started insisting that I invite them in to share my stuff with them. They wouldn't take no for an answer, and one of them had his foot in my doorway while both tried to push their way in. It became obvious to me that there was only one way they would get the message. When I was done with them, they clearly understood that they were not welcome at my door that night or any other night. When the policed showed up, one guy was still standing, barely, but his friend was out cold.

I was going to the pool hall in the evenings because there wasn't much else to do. There too I was making an effort to keep to myself, but it just wasn't working. I really did want to change my life, but it wasn't getting any easier—if anything, it was getting harder. I started to realize what an unbelievably wicked and tangled web I had woven, and I couldn't see any way out.

I had gone back out on the road, selling siding to support my addictions. Literally I'd be driving down the highway thanking Jesus for my last sale while filling up my cocaine pipe for my next fix. I knew it wasn't right, but I felt like I was stuck in my habits and lifestyle, and there was nothing I could do about it.

One day I parked my car in the back corner of a parking lot behind a semi truck and sat there all day, smoking pot and hash oil. I was really struggling, trying to figure out where my life was going and what I was going to do. It felt like the life I wanted to live was totally out of reach for me. I thought it was going to be easier, but I realized there was no way I could do it on my own. I had always taken care of my own problems and looked after myself, but this time I knew I needed help.

I called Ma Schroeder. "Ma," I said, "I need help. I can't do this."

She phoned a few people she knew, and the next day I got a call from Larson House, a dry-out centre in Saskatoon, saying they had a bed waiting for me. Normally there was a waiting list for people to get in, but Ma knew how to pull a few strings.

I took a cab there the following afternoon, but I was too scared to go in. The driver let me sit in the back seat and smoke a few joints while he took my bags to the front door. Then he came back to sit with me in the cab and, after a while, turned to me and said, "Young man, I've been in this business for many years and met a lot of people, and if anybody needs that building there it's you." When I was ready he would escort me to the door, but if I didn't want to go, he would put my bags back in the trunk. "It's your choice," he said.

I sat there for a few more minutes, trying to decide what to do. I didn't know if I could handle what was ahead, or if they could even help me. I wondered if I was maybe too far gone, just a hopeless case.

"Do you really think they can help me?" I asked.

"Yeah," he said, "I think they can."

CHAPTER 12

I spent the next three weeks in Larson House. They have a new building now, but when I entered it was an old, tall house converted into a dry-out centre. The unpleasant aroma made me feel even more like I had hit the bottom of the barrel.

In my first few days there all I did was sleep and try to get to the room where they served the meals.

After you're there a few days they give you a chore to do—mine was sweeping floors, which I thought was pretty low. On the second day of sweeping I opened a closet door to get a broom, and saw a guy sitting there in the closet, chugging back a bottle of Lysol cleaner. I watched for a couple of seconds, not believing what I was seeing. Then I slapped the bottle away from his face. "Are you nuts?," I said, "that stuff is going to kill you."

He looked at me and said, "Are you retarded? I'm not going to drink the whole bottle, only half of it."

I couldn't believe this guy chugging Lysol was asking me if I was retarded. I picked up my broom, closed the door and walked away.

In the first week I wasn't allowed to leave the building or have any visitors. They watched me pretty closely, to make sure I was okay. By the second week I was already starting to feel a little healthier. I was eating regular meals, and getting lots of sleep—I could feel my head clearing, and my body starting to feel stronger.

I had heard they held a dance every Friday evening at Calder Centre, the rehab place I would hopefully be moving to in a few weeks. Just about everyone from Larson House was going to the dance, and I wanted to go, too. It sounded like a fun diversion from the boring routines of the last couple of weeks.

I told the night shift counselor I wanted to go, but he said he wasn't giving me permission. We argued for a bit, and when I could see he wasn't going to budge I stormed up to my room, thinking he was being totally unreasonable and unfair. He followed me to my room, and kept trying to throw his weight around. He let me know that he was in charge, and that I needed to answer to him. I got mad and threw him against the wall and then out of my room.

Everyone at Larson House knew this counselor had a reputation for instigating arguments and scuffles. I don't know if he was let go or was moved to a different place, but I never saw him again after that. The next Friday evening I was allowed to go to the dance.

Other than the prescribed medication they gave me I didn't do any drugs while I was there. There were already a lot of drugs piled up in my system, and the medication they gave me just kept me on somewhat of an even keel. Physically I didn't seem to be reacting to the lack of drugs, but I could feel myself becoming volatile, emotionally. The fact that I was incredibly bored didn't help. I was sleeping 14 or 15 hours a day, playing cards or just talking to people—there wasn't much else to do. Ma and Pa came to visit me a few times and so did Pastor Ralph, but basically I just put in time and waited for the days to pass.

After three weeks at Larson House, I was moved to Calder Centre. My fears about being in rehab had pretty much subsided by then, and it felt to me like I was graduating. Finally, now I was going to start making some progress.

As soon as I arrived at Calder Centre I learned that one of the patients there was a penitentiary inmate who'd been doing time for a string of violent offences. He was at the Centre to take a drug rehab program so he could be considered for parole. He'd already been there for a couple of weeks when I arrived, and a few hours after I checked in he met me in the hall. He let me know that he knew all about me and my reputation as a fighter, but this was his place. He bumped into me and said, "Stay out of my f___ing way, you goof." I just ignored him and walked away, but I knew right then and there that the day would come when I would find out how tough he really was.

During the next week he kept going out of his way to insult me and call me out. One day, while I was sitting in the visitors lounge with Ma, he walked past us and started swearing at me and calling me a goof again. He grabbed the Lois L'Amour book I had been reading from me and said, "What do we have here? Another faggot cowboy book?" Then he ripped the book in half and threw it back in my face. I just stayed there, visiting with Ma, but in my mind I knew he had just sealed his fate. It was only a matter of time—there was only so much I could take.

There was a solarium on the third floor where we were allowed to smoke. I was there taking a break between sessions a couple of days later, relaxing and having a cigarette, when he walked in. He looked at me and said, "What the f___ do we have here?" He started to say something else, but I never heard what it was. I stood up and said, "That's the end of you!" As I stood up I kicked him and sent him flying backwards across the room. Then I kicked him all the way down the hallway to his room, leaving a trail of blood on the floor and walls the whole way. A couple of the other patients were crying and screaming, begging me to stop. "You're going to kill him!" they said. I could have, but I just rolled him into his room, closed the door and walked away.

I went straight to my room, packed my things and sat on my bed, waiting. I figured I was done at Calder Centre and would be heading off to jail. I waited there a whole hour until a counselor came into my room to apologize for letting things get out of hand. He said everyone knew what had been happening, and that the problem should have been dealt with earlier. He explained how they had actually been looking out for me, thinking I was the one who needed protection.

After talking with me and again saying he was sorry he helped me unpack my bag, and told me I could stay.

A few days later one of the doctors at the Centre told me that some people from the University of Saskatchewan wanted to talk to me. They were doing some research on addictions, and wanted me to be part of their study. I agreed, and they came to interview me. After talking with me for a while, they took some hair and blood samples, and asked me to fill out a 75-page questionnaire. They wanted to know everything about my drinking and drug habits—how much, how often, what kind, and when I had started. When they came back the next week after having processed all the information and samples I had given them they told me I was some sort of an anomaly. They said the hair and blood samples backed up everything I had told them, but it was humanly impossible for someone to put that amount of drugs and alcohol into his system and still be alive. They'd never seen anything like it.

They spoke to each other about my test results right there in front of me, which made me feel like a freak show again. I felt humiliated and used. Now that it was on paper, it was official: I was a freak. I started to wonder again if I was retarded.

They signed me up for their study, so for the next year I was to keep record of everything I took, which wasn't easy because I kept taking a lot. I had easy access to drugs, since no one at the Centre is locked in, and I was free to come and go as I pleased. You can get all the drugs you want just by talking to people at the AA and NA meetings (not everyone attends for the right reasons). After being at Calder Centre for a month, I knew the program had done nothing for me but reinforce in my mind that I was never going to change my addictive lifestyle. I was just too far gone.

I spent one night in the room of a girl just down the hall from the administration desk. The staff knew I was in there, but nobody did a thing about it. I got the feeling they didn't want to bother with me because they thought I was a lost cause.

On my first day out of the Centre I was driving along in my Buick LeSabre thinking, "The only reason I'm in this University study is because I'm a freak show, and they know I'm going to fail," so I decided I'd show them. I drove to the

Liquor Store, bought two 26ers of Kahlua, drank one right away and then drove around drinking the other one. I decided trying to change my old habits was hopeless, so why should I even bother making the effort?

After Calder Centre I moved into Ma and Pa Schroeder's guest room. That guest room was my home, on and off, for the next five years.

Through all that had happened I still had my old apartment in Lethbridge, and I started going back there regularly to reconnect with my old friends, and take care of business. I made the five-hour drive between Saskatoon and Lethbridge probably 100 times in the next year.

It seemed to me that everywhere I turned I was running into drugs. I was trying to get off cocaine, or to at least cut back a bit, but it obviously wasn't going well.

I didn't want to go back to selling siding, so I went to work for a friend in Saskatoon installing carpets instead. Like all my friends he was a drug addict. We worked hard together all week, making good money, and then on the weekends we hit the bars. One day after being paid we went to Confederation Park Bar, got into a routine fight, and then met a guy who asked us if we had ever done any cocaine. We asked why he wanted to know, and he said he was trying to get into dealing and had just come into possession of $2,500 worth of the stuff. He wanted to know if it was good quality. We smiled to each other and told him we could probably help him out. The three of us went over to his place and smoked every bit of it that night.

Shortly after that I went back to selling siding, and found myself back in the same old cycle of drinking and drugs. I was going back and forth between Saskatoon and Lethbridge almost every week. In Saskatoon I was selling siding and home renovations during the day and hustling in the bars and pool halls in the evenings. In Lethbridge I was helping a couple of friends with a grow-op, and keeping up with my old contacts. I was fighting a little less, and trying to cut down on the drinking and drugs, but it seemed that not a whole lot had changed in my life except that I was now attending church almost every Sunday.

I decided that, if nothing else, I would at least stop problem-solving. I was tired of hurting people and really wanted to put that part of my old life behind me. People were still contacting me and offering me jobs, but I turned them all down. It was tough, because it had been a lucrative business for me, but I was determined to make the change. But then one day, while I was staying at Ma and Pa Schroeder's, I got a phone call from a certain individual that I knew was high enough in the justice system that I should pay attention to what he had to say. Ma answered the phone, and when she told me it was the police I whispered to her to stay on the line and listen while I went to another phone. The gentleman on the phone told me about a very bad situation involving a few people who needed to be "taken care of." The things these men had done were horrible, and made my blood run cold. They were pure evil, and they needed to be stopped.

But I was no longer in the business. I tried to explain that to him, but he told me in no uncertain terms that if I didn't take care of this problem for him I would be looking at some hard jail time. He was well aware of my past and reminded me of some very serious situations that, if brought to light, might put me behind bars for a very long time.

After he hung up, I spent the next hour trying to decide what to do. The tentacles of corruption are far-reaching, and I finally decided that if I didn't do as he said, I was going to be in serious trouble. I didn't know what else to do, so, reluctantly, I asked Pa to open up the family safe where I had asked him to lock away my assortment of weapons a few months earlier. I could see that it broke Ma and Pa's hearts to watch me throw a duffle bag filled with "toys" into my car and drive away.

I had to leave right away because the job was out of the province and needed to be done within the next 24 hours. I was given an address and assured that the police would not be sent to the property until 30 minutes after the first gunshot had been reported.

After finishing that job I vowed to myself that, no matter what, I was out of the business for good.

Things hadn't been going well for me, but I still knew that what had happened to me that first day in Pastor Ralph's office was real. There was a God out there who had broken into my life and who loved me unconditionally. Something deep inside my heart kept telling me that I just needed to keep trusting him.

Month after month the same struggles kept repeating themselves. I would have a few good days, or maybe a good week or two, and I would start thinking I was finally making some real progress. But then I'd hit a tough spot, and whatever gains I had made would seem to be lost.

Something needed to change, and in the fall of 1989 the opportunity I needed came my way. Pastor Ralph told me that a group of young people from the church were going on a bus tour to visit a few Bible schools, and he thought it would be a good idea for me to go along. I was a lot older than everyone else, but I decided to join them anyway. We visited several schools in Manitoba and Saskatchewan over the next four days, and by the time we got back to Saskatoon I was convinced that I wanted to go to Bible school myself. The thought of studying the Bible and learning about God in that kind of a setting excited me. Rehab hadn't worked, but maybe this would; I had to give it a try.

When I told my friends in Lethbridge that I wouldn't be around for a while because I was going to be attending Bible school, they thought I was nuts. They just didn't get it. "Are you retarded?" they said.

There it was again. I hated that word, retarded. They would have never said it, even in a joking way, if they knew how much it bothered me, but no one knew. It was my personal struggle, my personal fear that I never shared with anyone.

The questions continued. "Have you snapped? Are you in trouble with the law? Did you get someone pregnant? Are you hiding from someone?" They knew I had become a Christian (whatever that meant), but this was going too far! They couldn't believe I was actually going to walk away from the drugs, power and sex, and go off to some school to learn about God. It didn't make any sense to them or anyone from my old life.

But in January, 1989, a year-and-a-half after I had dropped to my knees and prayed that prayer with Pastor Ralph, I started attending Bethany Bible Institute in the little town of Hepburn, about a half hour's drive north of Saskatoon. It was a Mennonite Brethren school, with about 150 students attending at that time. I couldn't pay for the tuition or even for room and board in the dorm, but thankfully there were some very good people from the church (and even a couple of friends from Lethbridge!) who helped me out. I thought it was kind

Pastor Ralph baptized me

of interesting that my drug-dealing friends were helping me pay my way through Bible school. Probably not many Bible school educations are supported with drug money, but mine was, at least in part. I also didn't have the credentials to get in, since I only had a grade nine education, but Pastor Ralph worked out some special arrangements for me through his affiliation with the school.

I was without a vehicle at that point in my life again, but Pa said I could drive his old farm truck to the school. It was Sunday evening, classes were scheduled to start the next morning, and I was getting really nervous about going. I waited until the last possible moment before I left. When I arrived I stopped the truck in the old hockey rink parking lot before the campus and said to myself, "Richard, do you really want to do this?" I was so scared that I was shaking, so I smoked a couple of joints to calm my nerves. Then, slowly, I drove up to the men's dorm.

I had been told where my room was, so I parked the truck, grabbed my stuff and went in. I could hear voices and laughter coming from behind some of the room doors, but I didn't see anyone—I was happy about that. I felt like such a fish out of water.

I found my room, which was right across the hall from the washroom, and went in. There was a single bed on each side of the room, a small closet at the foot of each bed, and a desk along the far wall, with a fluorescent light above it. Most of the guys in the dorm had a roommate, but for obvious reasons they decided to give me a room to myself. It looked quite comfortable and clean. The window swung open awning-style, but it didn't open wide enough to serve as an alternate exit. The only other issue was a fairly large gap under the door. I knew I would need to stuff that gap with a rolled-up towel sprayed with cologne to keep the smell of the drugs from escaping my room.

I unpacked my stuff and then just sat on my bed, trying to collect my thoughts and calm myself down. I had been sitting there for maybe 15 minutes when my door suddenly flew open and three guys came busting into my room. Pastor Ralph had been to the school a few days earlier to let the guys in the dorm know that I was coming. He told them about my background and personality, and that I was a fighter with a bit of an explosive temper. He had warned them not to surprise me or touch me, and to respect my space. I guess they hadn't gotten the message, but they were about to.

They were just trying to be friendly and were coming into my room to welcome me, but in my world any time someone barged into a room like that it meant something totally different. The instant my door opened, I was on my feet. I grabbed the first guy and threw him across the room into the desk. While he was still airborne I hit the second guy in the chest, knocking the wind out of him and sending him back out the door, sprawling into the third guy. The third guy never made it into the room, and I could see by the panicked look on his face and the way he threw up his arms and pleaded, "No, no, no," that I had probably misread the situation. They weren't there to fight.

I was still pretty wound up, so the first few words out of my mouth were more colourful than what is standard for Bible school dorm conversation. I think they got the message, that I hadn't exactly appreciated their actions. Then I mumbled a few words of apology, and they all left.

I angrily sat back down on my bed and thought, "This is just like the rehab centre. I can't even move into a Bible school dorm without getting into a fight!" I waited for someone to come and kick me out—I was sure that was coming. I sat there until 3:00 a.m., finally concluding that no one was coming to talk to me, so I went outside for a smoke. The whole place was quiet. The silence and the peace again blew me away; it was such a contrast to what I was used to.

I was still sure they were going to kick me out, but I decided they would probably wait for the morning before they would deal with me. I finished my smoke and tried to get some sleep.

A few hours later I heard noises outside my door, so I stuck my head into the hall and asked what was going on. A couple of guys told me they were going for breakfast, so I got myself ready and found my way to the cafeteria. At the buffet counter I saw hot and cold cereal, toast, coffee and juice. I knew I was going to have to do something about this, because that kind of a breakfast wasn't going to cut it for me.

I took my plate, piled a bit of food on it and found a table off to the side by myself. Word had gotten around that I had helped a few guys out of my room the night before, so I could see people looking at me and talking about me, or so I assumed. The cafeteria was noisy, but it was happy noise, with everyone talking and catching up on each other's lives after the Christmas break. They had all been together for at least one semester, some of them for two or three years already, so they all knew each other. There was a lot of laughing and joking around. So, as I sat at my table by myself I felt very out of place again. But I told myself that if they were going to let me stay I would make the most of this.

After I finished my breakfast Rick Schellenberg, the dean of students, asked me to come to the president's office. He introduced me to Cliff Jantzen, the school president. They were two of the most patient and forgiving men I have ever met, and they would also become two of the most influential men in my life for the next few years. I tested their patience many times, and they tested mine, too. They had rules, and they actually expected me to follow them!

They told me they had talked to the three guys I met the night before in the dorm, and the guys were sorry for coming into my room like that. The whole thing had just been a misunderstanding. They were hoping we could all just forget about it and move on. That was fine with me, and a lot better than I was expecting.

Rick and Cliff encouraged me to try to relax. They said their doors would always be open, and I could come to talk with them whenever I wanted. They explained that they weren't used to me just like I wasn't used to them, but if we tried to work together we could do this. They gave me permission to get up and leave class or take a break any time I needed to. They told me they would do whatever they could to help me adjust to life at the Bible school.

"Is there anything else you need?" they asked.

"Well, now that you mention it," I said, "for breakfast I'm used to having two poached eggs, brown toast and hash browns."

Every weekday morning after that, the kitchen ladies handed me a plate with my own breakfast of eggs, toast and hash browns. On the weekends, since there was only a skeleton kitchen staff, breakfast was downsized to cold cereal and toast, so I went to the restaurant in town to have my own breakfast there.

CHAPTER 13

I walked around in a state of shock for the rest of that first morning. I just wandered around and looked at everything, and watched what was happening. What I saw blew me away. This was the most innocent and gentle group of people I had ever been around. They were happy and joking around with each other. There was no swearing, no one was smoking, and even the roughhousing was just child's play. There was a wholesomeness that just blew me away; I had never seen anything like it.

I knew I would have to adapt to a whole new world. I had to learn that they could be sarcastic and not mean anything by it. If someone called you a goof, you didn't kick the crap out of him. It was okay for people to reach out and touch you. You didn't need to be on your guard every second of the day and be ready to fight every time someone approached you. I knew it would be a challenge, but I wanted to find a way to fit into this place.

Lunch that first day was another reminder that fitting in wouldn't be easy. Outside the cafeteria I tried to get past what I thought was a group of people milling about when a kid half my age stopped me, and said I should go to the back of the line. I hadn't even realized there was a line—I thought these people were just standing around talking. At breakfast there were less people, so you could just walk up to the buffet and get your food, and I assumed it worked the same for lunch, too.

I felt embarrassed, and walked to the back of the line where I stood behind a couple of girls. After a few minutes a guy came along and cut right in front of me, which I didn't appreciate at all.

"Excuse me," I said, "are you stupid? You can't butt in front of me."

He gave me a look like I was an idiot, and said, "These girls were saving a place for me, weren't you girls?"

The girls hesitated, glanced at me, and then looked back at him. They were clearly nervous and not quite sure what they should say. It was obvious he had just tried to blow me off, so I grabbed him by his shirt and threw him off to the side.

Suddenly, it was very quiet and everyone was staring at me again. I stood there for a few seconds, even more embarrassed, and then left the line and walked back to my room. I was mad at myself for losing my temper. "I'm not like anyone here," I thought. And I found it humiliating to stand in line for my meals like a little kid. I was used to going wherever I wanted, whenever I wanted, and eating whatever I felt like eating. I was used to people clearing out of my way because they were afraid of me, and nobody ever questioned me or told me what to do.

Here no one knew who I was, and the rules of the game were completely different. It was going to take some getting used to.

I didn't go back to classes that afternoon; I just walked out of town along the railway tracks to calm myself down. I wasn't in the mood to go through anything like that again for suppertime, so I ate at a restaurant in town. It hadn't been a good first day, but I decided I would try to do better tomorrow.

Over the next few days things started to improve. I learned my way around, and got familiar with the routines. Most importantly, I started to make a few friends. It was still awkward for me, and probably even more awkward for them, but I started to believe that maybe I could make this work. I really wanted to make it work.

There were still a couple more incidents with the guys in the dorm those first few weeks. There was one kid who was being picked on, and although it was all in fun I could see that it was bothering him. I had always stuck up for the underdog, so one afternoon I grabbed the guy who was teasing him and threw him up against the wall a couple of times. I held him up against the wall by his throat and told him that if he liked picking on people then maybe he should try picking on me.

I got called into the dean's office for that one. Rick told me quite sternly that I couldn't be doing things like that. That just wasn't the way they handled their problems around here.

A few days later there was another situation involving a big guy who had played a bit of semi-pro football and had even earned a tryout with the BC Lions as a lineman. He thought he was pretty tough, and couldn't understand how a little guy like me could be stronger than him. He was a friend of the guy that I had just tuned in a couple of days before, and he started bragging to a few of the other guys that he was going to set me straight. That evening in the dorm, he confronted me, with about 35-40 guys gathered around to see what would happen. The mood was calm, not at all like the fights I used to have behind the nightclub. These guys had heard I was a fighter, and were curious to see how this would turn out.

"I know you're fast," the big guy said, "but if I grabbed you, I could bust you."

I said, "Okay, how would you grab me?"

He explained that if he put me in a headlock I wouldn't be able to get out of it. I invited him to test that theory if he really wanted to. He smiled and came over to put his arm around my neck. A couple of seconds later, he was lying on the ground gasping for breath.

I thought that would be the end of it, but he didn't seem to be the quickest learner. After he got his breath back he stood up and said, "Okay, if I put you in a bear hug there's no way you could get out if it."

I let him come up behind me and wrap his arms around me. He squeezed as hard as he could and lifted me off the ground. When he said he was ready I instantly thrust forward and drove my rear into his midsection, bending him over. In the same motion I instantly straightened my body out and slammed the back of my head into his chin. Again he was lying on the floor, writhing in pain. It had taken me about one second to get out of his bear hug. I felt bad about hurting him, but he asked for it. There were no more incidents with him after that.

One day I decided to turn the unused closet in my room into a sauna. I didn't have a roommate, so I didn't think it would be a problem. I covered the walls with plastic garbage bags, brought in a chair, and then plugged a couple of electric kettles into an extension cord that I ran under the door. It was fairly simple, but it worked quite well. When I needed to unwind I would fill up the kettles and go sit in there for a while. Some of the other guys thought it was a good idea, and several more closet saunas popped up in the dorm.

Classes were beginning to be exciting and fascinating, but also a challenge, not only for me, but for the teachers who had to put up with my endless questions. I could tell they were getting frustrated with me, but there was just so much I wanted to know, so much I needed to know. Because it was all brand new to me, sometimes I stumbled over the simplest lessons, but as I started to learn I just got hungrier and hungrier for more. I needed to know if what I was hearing was true. I was trying to change my life, and I had to know if I was on the right path.

Often in class I felt like I had been shortchanged. I knew I had the intellectual smarts to grasp the concepts and to understand what was being taught, but I didn't have the book smarts. My reading and writing skills were way behind the other students. I found that frustrating, and hard to deal with.

This was a Mennonite school, and Mennonites, I learned, are known to be pacifists. They believe that the Bible teaches you to be kind to your enemies. If someone hits you on one cheek you should turn the other cheek and let him hit you there, too. That was a new one for me. I figured that if someone was trying to hit you, it made more sense to hit him first, and to hit him hard enough that he wouldn't be able to get up and hit you back. I couldn't grasp that whole "turning the other cheek" concept.

I could never sit in a classroom with someone behind me. I always had to sit at the back of the class, against the wall so I could see everything that was going on. I kept reminding myself that this was a safe place, but still I could never let anyone get behind me. It had been a matter of survival for many years already, and I wasn't about to let my guard down—I couldn't. It might have seemed a little strange to the other students at first, but after a while they got used to it.

For my whole life I firmly believed everyone was either a friend or a foe, with no middle ground. Either someone was in my inner circle of trusted friends or they were a rival who could never be trusted. Here at school I didn't know anyone well enough to trust them, so naturally I saw everyone as a foe. When I told Rick Schellenberg about this feeling he suggested I study the pictures of all the current students in the school yearbook. As I got to know the other students, he said, I should try to think of one thing I liked about each of them. It was harder for some than for others, but eventually over the next few months I was able to come up with one good thing that I could say about everyone. Some of them sang well, some were generous with their time or their money, some were really patient or said encouraging things to others, and some of them helped me with my assignments. One girl found out what kind of cologne I liked and bought me some when I ran out. After a while I found I was starting to like everyone here.

Cliff Jantzen, the school president, supported and encouraged me in so many amazing ways. A few parents of some of the other students expressed some concerns about me living in the dorm, but he backed me all the way. He invited me into his home quite a few times, where we had long conversations about how big and how gracious God is. He encouraged me to think big. "What could God do through you?" he would ask. He told me to listen to my heart and do whatever I wanted to do. He seemed like such a wise and godly man. After our visits I sometimes went away thinking to myself, "How can a person get to be like him?"

The highlight of every day for me was the morning chapel service, and especially the singing—I didn't ever want it to stop. I'd always loved music, but there was more to it than that. Just being in that place, worshipping God together with 150 others was amazing! That's when I knew in my heart that I had discovered something real. I was still doing a lot of drugs, and sometimes I was too stoned to make it to my first class, but I always forced myself to get to chapel, no matter what kind of shape I was in. Sometimes I came in staggering.

There were a lot of talented musicians and singers at the school— Mennonites are known for their singing, and music was a big part of Bethany life. A few smaller groups sang in chapel services (and sometimes went out to different churches in the area), but the school was really well-known for its choirs. I loved listening to the choir. I'd never heard music like that before, and I thought it was beautiful.

Sometimes when the choir was practicing I would stand out in the hall next to the music room and listen. One day the choir conductor caught me standing with my ear against the door, and told me I should come in and join them. I told him that he really didn't want me in there, because I couldn't sing. "I like to sing," I said, "I just can't."

"Sure you can," he said. "Everyone can sing. With a little practice you'll fit right in." He told me he'd never kicked anyone out of choir because they couldn't sing.

"Not yet," I said, "but that's because you haven't heard me."

I kept trying to tell him he was making a serious mistake, but he wouldn't listen. Eventually I gave in, and took my place in the choir. As soon as I started to sing I could sense the uneasiness around me. After just a few minutes he called me over. "You were right," he said. "You can't sing." That was the one and only choir practice I ever attended.

I kept hanging around the music room whenever I could, because I found the music comforting. There was a lot of turmoil inside of me, and I found that the music calmed me down. I was trying my best to cut back on the drugs, and listening to music seemed to help when things got tough. Sometimes when some of the pianists were practicing I would lay on top of the big grand piano while they played. They were really good about it, and continued to play with me lying there. Sometimes when they were done practicing I would ask them to keep playing a little longer. Everyone was so good to me. The love and the support I was starting to feel was beyond anything I could have imagined. I didn't know people could care that much.

One of the good friends I made at school was Victor. He played the saxophone. Often he would come to my room at night to play the sax, and talk to me until I fell asleep. Then he'd turn off the light and quietly leave.

At some time during that semester I noticed that being in this place where I felt so loved and supported was starting to have an impact on me. I was doing way less drugs, I was talking differently, and I found myself being much more patient when things didn't go my way—I was starting to change. I was really starting to change! It was exciting! "This is crazy!" I thought.

Victor had the nicest car on campus—a Camaro IROC-Z28. I saw it in the parking lot one day and discovered who owned it. He let me take it for a ride, and we started to become friends after that.

Victor was a big Edmonton Oilers fan, and I told him I knew a guy who could hook us up with some game tickets. So one afternoon, three of us decided we should head to Edmonton to catch a game, but it was starting in 4 hours and it's a five-and-a-half-hour drive from Hepburn to Edmonton, normally. I told Victor that if he would hand me the car keys, I'd get us there on time. We were in our seats for the opening face off. We stayed overnight and got back just in time for supper the next day.

Victor was not only a devoted hockey fan, he was also a very good hockey player, and was top scorer on Bethany's team in a Saskatoon rec-hockey league. Because of this status he usually got some "special attention" from the other team. I didn't think it was always fair the way the opposing players checked him and tried to rough him up, but Victor didn't seem bothered by it—he said it was just part of the game. But I would get pretty upset sometimes. I'd stand up against the glass as close to the ice as I could get and yell threats to the other players and offer my opinion on how the refs were calling the game.

Once when I was watching a game with a pool hall buddy Victor got punched in the back of the head after scoring a goal. My friend and I had come prepared for just such an incident. We each had a few hockey pucks in our pockets, and when the player who had punched Victor came skating back across the ice we started throwing them at him. Things escalated quite quickly from there, and somehow a small riot developed. The game was called, and after I had kicked in the ref's dressing room door I was given a police escort back to the school. Again, Rick Schellenberg told me to cool it saying, "That's not the image the school is trying to portray."

The weekends were pretty much open for students to do whatever they wanted. Most of them stayed on campus, either working on assignments or catching up on sleep, but the students who lived close enough to home would often go there for the weekends. One day Ma and Pa Schroeder told me they were going away for a few weeks so I was welcome to have a few of the guys over at their house for a weekend to watch some movies. They would even leave some snacks for us. That sounded like fun, so I invited a bunch of guys from the dorm to come into Saskatoon for the weekend. When we got to Ma and Pa's condo we found out that their daughter who had been checking in on the place had locked both the doorknob and the deadbolt, and I only had a key for the doorknob. I didn't feel like disappointing myself or the guys with me, who had really been looking forward to this. Besides, there were snacks inside.

"Stand back," I said. It took three kicks, because the frame was steel, but I eventually got us in. The door and frame were completely destroyed, and when we left to go back to school I taped a piece of paper across the doorway with the words "DO

NOT CROSS!" written on it. It sounds ridiculous now, but at the time it seemed to make perfectly good sense. We had a lot of fun that weekend.

About the only other time that I got in any real trouble that semester was when I blew up a cherry bomb in the library. Victor and I were making a bit too much noise one day, and a couple of guys that I thought were a bit preppy told us to be quiet. Just for fun, we decided to get them back. So a couple of days later, when the two guys were studying together in the library, we pulled off our plan. First, I told the librarian there was a phone call for her in the student lounge. As soon as she left Victor handed me the cherry bomb, I lit it and threw it under the guys' chairs. It was only about the size of a golf ball, but Victor obviously knew how to build a cherry bomb.

The result was everything we had hoped for. The bomb went off and they flew backwards off their chairs and hit the floor. Unfortunately, one of them hit his head on the table on the way down, but it didn't seem like he was hurt too badly. Of course, we were called into the dean's office to explain ourselves. I said it was Victor's bomb and that, although I had been a willing participant, it was his scheme. I'm not sure they believed me, but Victor was the one who had to pay $50 to repair the damage to the carpet.

The progress I made in cutting back on cocaine that first semester was nothing short of amazing. I think there were only three times that I did cocaine in the four months I was there which, for me, was incredible! I was still smoking pot fairly regularly, but considering the amount I was used to doing I thought I had made real progress. I usually tried to smoke my joints outside, or at least by my window. But one morning I was so upset about something that I went down to the furnace room, smoked three big joints and blew the smoke right into the furnace. Good pot smells like skunk when you smoke it, so all morning people were looking around the dorm for the skunk.

I learned a lot that first semester. I learned about God and the stories in the Bible, but most of all I learned how to live with people. It was an introduction to living a Christian life and getting along with others.

I remember being blown away by the way young people there were making life decisions and planning for their future. That was a brand new concept for me. To this point I had never seriously thought to myself, "What am I going to be when I grow up?" I had just worked at surviving day to day and not thinking much beyond that. But suddenly I was faced with the possibility that there might be something in store for me for the future. God might have a plan for my life. That thought was exciting, but also scary.

When the semester ended, I was convinced that I wanted to come back. I believed that if I could come back for a full year I would be able to not only kick my addictions, but I would be able to get a handle on this new life I wanted to be living. The hope inside of me was beginning to grow into a powerful force. I finally had something to live for. I had a reason to keep trying.

CHAPTER 14

That summer I went back to Lethbridge, started selling siding again and also hooked up with a few friends who were doing construction work. I planned to make a little money, get through the summer, and then go back to Bible school in the fall. I really felt that if I could get another year of Bible school under my belt I would be on my way, and there would be no turning back.

I had done really well cutting back on the drugs while I was in Bible school, but as soon as I was back with my old friends I fell right back into my old habits. I stayed away from cocaine, but went right back to smoking pot and hash every day. In that environment there really wasn't anything else I felt I could do. I knew that if I tried to cut back any more, I would just fail and get discouraged. Besides, in my mind it wasn't that big of a deal. I felt like I had already made some huge strides and I was feeling good about how far I had come. I decided I would just take it easy through the summer and then go back to school in the fall.

After work one day, a few of us were sitting around in a bar when a guy came around wanting to buy some drugs, so I slipped him a little bit of black hash. About a week later I ran into him again, and sold him a bit more. That was a mistake. The guy was a narc, and I got busted for trafficking. How ironic, that in all those years when I had been seriously dealing drugs there had been very few actual run-ins with the law, but now that I was honestly trying to straighten out my life, one careless move had landed me in some pretty serious trouble. My court date was set for October.

I tried going to church a few times that summer, but I felt like I didn't fit in. It was obvious to me that I was still very different than the people there. I was becoming a different person on the inside, but the way I was living on the outside hadn't changed much at all. After trying a couple of churches I gave up, and just hung out with my friends instead.

In the bars and clubs people still saw me as the same old Rick. I kept trying to tell them that I had changed, but it was clear that no one really believed it. Everyone still treated me the same, and still expected me to fight.

In Lethbridge at that time there were four of the toughest, meanest guys around—they called themselves the Wrecking Crew—who I heard had been causing damage all over southern Alberta for about a year. Everyone was afraid of them, for good reason. They were all big boys, having played a bit of junior football together, and I was also told they had a racist flare. I was really upset when I found out they had taken a drunk Native guy out to a farmyard to bullwhip him.

One night when I was leaving the pool hall I saw them jumping on some cars in the parking lot, just damaging people's vehicles for no reason. They liked to provoke people because they knew that no one would come after them. They'd been in trouble with the police a few times, but they'd never received anything more than a slap on the wrist. As I left that evening they were jumping on the hood of a small car that someone was trying to drive away. The driver looked terrified. I didn't fight them that evening because I didn't think the time was right, but in my mind I knew that one day soon they were going to get it.

About a week later I was back at the same pool hall when someone came running in screaming, "The Wrecking Crew is beating up somebody outside!" When I heard the word "somebody," I knew it was just one person against the four of them, and that didn't seem right. My blood started to boil, and I decided it was time to take care of these guys once and for all. I wasn't in the habit of looking for fights, and really hadn't wanted anything to do with these guys. It's not that I was afraid of them; I just couldn't be bothered. But the stories I'd heard about the Wrecking Crew and the carnage they always left behind stirred up that old rage inside me. These guys were bad news, and someone had to stop them.

I managed to appear calm on the outside, but on the inside I was steaming—this wasn't going to be pretty. I told my friend Scott, who was working there, to get everyone in the pool hall to go outside and make a big circle around the Wrecking Crew, so they couldn't get away. Once everyone was outside I walked into the middle of the circle where the Wrecking Crew was beating up a pizza delivery guy. He was a tall, skinny kid, who wasn't fighting back at all. He was just leaning back over a car, and they were roughing him up and punching him in the gut.

I walked up behind the guy who was doing the punching and gave him a right hook to the jaw. I felt his jawbone break and he crumpled to the ground. I had caught them off guard, and as soon as the other guys realized what was happening they turned and tried to make a run for it. I grabbed the second guy just as he started to turn around, reached over the top of his head, grabbed him by the eye sockets and camel-fisted him across the bridge of his nose. I felt the bones in his face crush, and when he fell to the ground I stomped on his face. In the same motion I chopped the third guy in the throat and then punched him in the ear. He was knocked out cold.

All of this happened in less than 10 seconds. I piled the three guys up on top of each other and then turned to look for the fourth member of the crew. He was trying to get away, but no one was letting him through the circle. My friends were taunting him, saying, "You're going to get it, man. Look what happened to your buddies. You're next."

He was the biggest one of the bunch, probably outweighing me by 100 lbs. I walked over to him, and he started begging and pleading for me not to hurt him. He was shaking and crying. "We'll never do this again," he said. "Don't hurt me, please don't hurt me."

"You don't understand, buddy," I said. "I'm not only going to hurt you; I'm going to destroy you. I'm going to crush you and break your legs. You will never be able to touch anyone again."

"I hope you're going to fight back," I said. "The other guys didn't, and it's kind of boring that way." He just stood there shaking, so I took him by the hands and raised his fists up to his face. "Come on," I said, "let's go."

The second he moved I punched him with everything I had in me. I caught him square in the face. I felt his face explode, and blood splattered everywhere. He fell back over the hood of a car, and as he was sliding off I kicked him in the leg and saw the bone snap. I kicked him a few more times while he was on the ground, and then threw him on the pile with the other guys.

For the next few minutes, any time one of them moved or made a sound, I hit him again. Finally the police showed up. "Langlais, you can stop now," they said. I ignored them, and threw a few more punches into the pile. They warned me a couple more times, and then pulled a gun. "Langlais, that's enough," they said again.

"I think you're right," I said. Then I threw one last punch into the pile, turned and walked away.

That was the end of the Wrecking Crew. People in Lethbridge today still talk about that fight.

Other than that incident it was kind of a boring summer. I was helping some friends run a grow-op, selling siding and drugs, scamming people and getting into the occasional fight. It was the same old life I'd always known, and yet something about it felt strangely empty. I found myself yearning to get back to Bible school and back to my new life. There was so much more I wanted to learn, so many more questions that needed answers. In that way it was a confirmation for me that I was on the right path. There were two very distinct and different lives I was living: one was beginning to have less and less appeal, while the other had me longing for more.

Partway through the summer I picked up a stolen car. A buddy of mine had stolen it, but he was getting nervous about driving it around, so I took it over from him. I got caught in a high-speed chase a little while later, and the stolen car charges were added to the trafficking charges for my court date coming up in October.

Then summer was over and it was time to go back to Bible school, but I hadn't saved any money, so I wasn't sure I would be able to attend. At the last minute the school phoned and told me someone had paid all my expenses for the next semester. Classes were starting in a couple of days, so I went down to a local car lot and helped myself to a brand new Mercury Sable. "Nice car," people said when I got to Hepburn. "Thanks," I said.

After a few weeks I was feeling guilty, and confessed that I had stolen the car. The owner of the car lot decided to not press charges. He was the dad to one of my friends in Lethbridge, and decided to just treat it as a minor error in judgment on my part. I was very thankful. Going into court with another stolen car charge would not have been a good thing.

I was excited about getting back into classes. This time I knew what to expect, and I felt like I belonged. I had high hopes for the year and I was looking forward to learning more about the Bible. I really enjoyed the classes, but the daily chapels were still the highlight for me.

In October I had to leave for my court appearance. I beat the stolen car rap, but was found guilty on the trafficking charge and spent the next two months in the Lethbridge jail. Rick Schellenberg drove me there, and on the way I remember praying, "Hey God, I'll see you when I get back out."

During the years I had been bouncing I had, at one time or another, had a run-in with quite a few of the guys who were doing time in the jail, so it seemed that almost everyone there knew who I was. I even recognized a guard who I had thrown out of a club a few years ago because he and some of his friends had gotten out of hand. They thought they were pretty tough and were throwing their weight around, so I had helped them out the door. He must have remembered the incident well, because after supper on my first day in jail he walked into the

TV room where some of us were sitting around, and he looked at me and started to laugh. "Hey everyone," he said, "if you like to dance, this guy will be your dance partner. He's a dance instructor."

"Dance" is the jail word for fight, and he was trying to set me up. I looked at him and said, "If I remember right, I bounced you and your girlfriends right out of my place one night." His face turned red, and then he walked away. He was a tough, stocky guard, but not very intelligent. He could have gotten himself into trouble there.

The next morning when I went to the dining hall for breakfast I noticed everyone keeping their distance from me. When I walked over to a table and put my tray down, the two guys already sitting there got up and left. A minute or two later my roommate came over, asking if he could sit with me. "Right there," I said, pointing across the table. Then I asked him, "What's going on?" I thought maybe I was a marked man, and that they were planning on coming after me.

"No," he said, "it looks like you're the new man on the block."

I didn't have to do anything; my reputation had done it for me. I honestly thought I was going to have to splat the first guy who came at me, but I never had to fight anyone the whole time I was there. It was a picnic; everyone left me alone. The guard had tried to set me up, but letting everyone know who I was had backfired and worked to my advantage.

The jail was run by a guy named Kenny. I knew he was a tough character, and he had heard the same about me. We had one brief conversation where things were settled, and there were never any issues between us. He was cool about it.

While I was in jail I got lots of cards and letters from people in the church and from my Bible school friends. That encouraged me a lot. I prayed to God every day, and I knew that he was real.

When I got out of jail I was put on probation, on condition that I couldn't leave the Bible school campus. That was hard, and there were a few times when I didn't exactly comply with the letter of the law. There were still way too many opportunities to get into trouble or to go out and just have some fun.

While I was gone I had missed a few months of classes, but that really didn't matter that much. I wasn't planning on writing any exams anyway. I hadn't been put in any kind of a program at the school—I was just attending classes and doing whatever papers and reading assignments that I felt like doing. I was learning at my own pace and in my own way. But I was learning a lot. I was hungry, and was taking it all in.

At Christmas break the dorm emptied out and everyone went home for the holidays. I still wasn't allowed to leave campus, so I would be spending Christmas break right there. The first night was okay, but the second day of being alone was too much to take. That night, I decided to borrow a car from the school and go into Saskatoon for a couple of days. I figured I'd spend Christmas at the pool hall, hustling pool and hooking up with some old friends. I thought I was strong enough to handle whatever temptations came my way, but I was so wrong. I got into some cocaine and, over the next couple of days, fell off the wagon, hard. I told myself I had been doing so well that I deserved a little treat for the holidays. But once I got started I couldn't stop.

I went back to the dorm after a couple of days, and a little while later Rick Schellenberg came to my room to talk with me. He knew I had taken off, and wanted to know how I was doing. I told him the whole story, including the fact that I now owed someone $350 for some drugs. I didn't have any money to pay off my debt at the moment, but I knew I could easily make what I needed playing pool. Rick didn't think it was a good idea for me to go back there, so he went to the bank, took out the money and gave it to me. I felt bad for what I had done. I felt like I had let myself and everyone else down again.

The final semester in spring had its challenges, and I still got myself into trouble a few more times than I should have, but I stuck it out and learned a lot. In the classroom things were starting to make more sense, and I felt like I was getting a handle on what it meant to be a Christian. I was learning more all the time, especially how to relate to people around me in a more gentle, loving way. Most importantly, I was learning how to read my Bible and pray. When things got really tough that's what I did.

Back in my first semester at Bethany an idea had started to formulate in my mind, and now that my time at the school was coming to a close I started thinking more about it: I wanted to start a street ministry for hardcore adults in Saskatoon. I was becoming convinced that God wanted me to do this. I had no idea how I was going to get it going or where the money would come from, and I didn't have any idea how to run a ministry, but I felt like it was what I should be doing.

After school was over, I went back to Lethbridge to try earning some money. I was planning on getting married in the next year to a girl I had met in Bible school. We were going to live in Saskatoon where I would figure out a way to open an inner-city ministry. That summer I visited a few street ministries in several cities across western Canada to see what people were doing, and to get some ideas. I watched what was happening at the ministries, talked to the directors, and asked each one for a copy of their constitution and operating policies. I wanted to learn everything I could about running a ministry.

It looked like every ministry I visited was a reflection of the director's personality and background. They just did whatever they were good at. Some places were just simple soup kitchens, some offered clothing and a place to sleep, and others were just a place to get a cup of coffee and talk to someone. Ministries that were Christian and those with no religious affiliation seemed almost alike—if you took out the word "Christ" there really wasn't much difference. They were all about meeting basic human needs and giving dignity, and that's what I wanted to do. I thought that if Jesus was around, that's what he would do.

After visiting about a dozen ministries and drop-in centres, I realized that if I was going to run a successful ministry it would need to based on who I was and what I could do. I wasn't a counselor or a pastor, so I would have to take more of a hands-on approach. The name "Hands On" stuck in my mind—I liked that. I thought to myself, "What would have made a difference for me when I was on the street? What would have made my life more positive, even in little ways?"

I didn't think there would be any churches interested in supporting me, but I believed with all my heart that this was what I was being called to do. It seemed that every time I mentioned the idea to someone, that person would encourage me to do it. More than that, I believed that God knew my heart. He knew that I really wanted to help out those who were most in need. I still had doubts and fears, and there were still questions in my mind. Would I be able to stay out of trouble? Would doing something like this help me keep my life on track? Could I do something that was bigger than me? I hoped the answer to all those questions was yes.

Chapter 15

I spent the next year going back and forth between Lethbridge and Saskatoon again. I was living and working in Lethbridge, but the girl I was engaged to was finishing up her last year of Bible school, so I travelled to see her quite often. My life in Lethbridge was pretty much the same as it had always been. I was selling siding, hanging out with the guys, doing lots of drugs and hustling in the pool halls and nightclubs. I was off the hard drugs, but I was still smoking pot and hash every day. I didn't think anything of it; it was just what we did. But that year I felt like I was just putting in time, waiting to move on to the next stage of my life.

In June, 1992 I said goodbye to my Lethbridge friends and moved to Saskatoon, and in August I got married. It felt like that summer I was finally turning a corner, putting my old life behind me for good. I was still good friends with the guys back in Lethbridge, and that would never change, but the lifestyle I had been living up to that point was over now. It was a new start, and my life was starting to level out.

After the wedding my wife and I moved into a highrise apartment in downtown Saskatoon, and I settled in to my new life as a married man. It was great! I was in love and feeling like I was on the road to bigger and better things. I was looking forward to opening Hands On Street Ministry, and I was very excited about what God had in store for me for the future.

When I had first started thinking about setting up a street ministry I thought it would just be something I would do myself, with the help of a few friends. But as word about the ministry spread around to various churches in Saskatoon people started donating money and offering their support.

Several local businesses offered to supply food and other basic necessities. One day a friend gave me a cheque for $5,000 and said it was time to get started.

Hands On needed a building, so I started looking around on 20th Street, in the heart of Saskatoon's inner city. Then one day I got a message delivered to me from a guy named Bernie, a well-known personality in the crime world. He was a rounder, which meant that he dabbled in a little bit of everything. He was a street hustler and a businessman, but in Saskatoon he was best known for his porn shop. Although we had never met face to face we knew of each other, and I had heard that he was a fair man. Talk on the street was that he had a hard side, but that his word could be trusted.

He was renting out the space above his porn shop to a poker and strip club called The Pink Flamingo. The owners of the club were three months behind on their rent and were being hard to deal with, so Bernie sent word to me through the street that I should come to see him, because he had a proposition for me. I thought he meant that he wanted me to come over to solve his problem, so I sent word back that I was no longer in the business. He returned a message that started with, "Hey buddy...." I decided it would be wise to see what he wanted, because if I didn't the next message was going to start with, "Hey something else...." Bernie was known as the King of 20th Street, so I knew that if I was going to set up there I would need to talk to him at some point anyway. This was as good a time as any.

When I met him in his office he described the difficulties he was having with the upstairs tenants, and he told me about the several thousand square feet of space that might be coming available. He had heard I was looking for a place for my ministry, and wanted to make me an offer. After talking about the situation for a few minutes I said that, since these tenants were being so uncooperative and were three months behind on rent, it only seemed fair to me that, if I could convince them to leave, I should get three months of free rent myself.

"Go to work," Bernie said.

Immediately I ran upstairs and asked the gentlemen running the place for the keys. They wanted to know why, so I informed them that they would be leaving immediately. They said they had no intention of leaving then or at any time, for that matter. Push came to shove, and shove we did. An hour later they were limping out with whatever they could carry—everything they left behind was mine.

I went back downstairs and gave the keys to Bernie, who handed them right back to me. "I'll be looking for some rent in four months," he said.

Putting a Christian ministry above a porn shop honestly wasn't an issue in my mind. I was going to be ministering to hardcore street people, so the location actually made good sense to me. Any volunteers I had coming from churches could just use the back door to avoid embarrassment.

Over the next couple of weeks I went to work setting up Hands On. The layout of the building was actually quite good for what I wanted. The front door was at street level, and from there three short flights of switchback stairs led up to a 12' x12' foyer. Since the place had been used for activities that weren't exactly legal it had been divided into separate rooms, with locking doors all off the foyer area. I didn't really need the locks on the doors, but I decided to leave the rooms as they were and use each of them for different purposes. The small room facing the street would be my office, so I could keep an eye on who was there or who was coming and going, and always be aware of who was coming up the stairs. One of the larger rooms off to the side would be turned into a sitting room. There would also be a clothing room where people could pick up used clothes for free. The largest area would be used for eating and working out. I brought in some mats and punching bags, trying to model the room after what I remembered from Tuny's martial arts studio in Prince George. I wanted it to be a place where the hardcores would feel comfortable. Besides, I was a fighter, and I knew that if Hands On was going to be a success it would need to be a reflection of who I was.

In less than a month Hands On was open, and within a few days there was a regular flow of ex-cons, drug addicts, prostitutes and homeless people coming through the doors. Quite a few of the regulars were First Nations people who had moved to Saskatoon from the reserves in northern Saskatchewan. Life on the streets was hard, and those who came into Hands On seemed to be thankful for the food and conversation, but mostly they just appreciated having a safe place to relax for a while. I liked watching the really hardcore guys and ex-cons who liked to work out their aggression by swinging and kicking at the heavy bags. I felt like I could relate to them.

Hands On was up and running, and for the next few months more and more people came through the doors. It was exactly what I had envisioned. I knew I couldn't help everyone, but I also knew I was making a difference for at least a few people. I talked openly about Jesus and about God's love, but I didn't preach at anyone about changing their life—that wouldn't do anything but drive people away. I just accepted everyone for who they were, tried to give them a sense of dignity and did my best to show the love of Jesus in any way I could. I knew my actions spoke volumes.

One afternoon, after Hands On had been open a couple of months, I heard a commotion and looked up to see a group of six kids coming through the door—five boys and one girl. The oldest looked to be about 11 or 12 years old, and the youngest was maybe six. Their eyes widened as they looked around the room. "Wow!" they said, and before I could stop them, they ran over to the heavy bags and started hitting them.

I walked over and said as sternly as I could, "You guys get out of here; this place ain't for kids." I escorted them over to the door and told them to get lost.

The next day, right after school, all six of them were back again. They saw the sandwiches and other food sitting on the counter that were meant for the hardcores, and said, "Hey, you got anything for us to eat?"

"No," I said. "Get out of here!"

"Can we play?" they asked.

"Can't you guys understand English?" I said. "Go home! I don't even like kids."

They turned around and ran back down the stairs, laughing like they had just played a trick on me or something.

I couldn't believe it when they showed up again the next day. "Got any cookies?" they asked.

"Are you kids crazy?" I said. "I thought I told you to get lost." They just stood there, staring at me and smiling. It was quite obvious to me they weren't going anywhere.

"Stay here," I said. Then I ran downstairs to Bernie's. "Hey Bernie," I asked, "Do you have any cookies?"

It just so happened that Bernie had recently come into possession of an entire truckload of cookies. I didn't ask how he had gotten them, and he didn't offer any explanation. It was probably best if I didn't know.

"Do I have cookies?" He said. "Come 'ere." He went down the hall and unlocked a storage room door. Inside the room were cases and cases of cookies, stacked one on top of another. He took down a case and opened it up. "Help yourself," he said. I reached in and grabbed a couple of bags. "Take the whole thing," he said.

I went back upstairs and handed each of the kids a few bags of cookies. I figured this would keep them happy for a while. "Now get lost," I told them. I was hoping that would be the last I saw of the little brats, but I was wrong. The cookies idea had backfired. The next day after school there must have been at least 50 kids who showed up, all of them asking for cookies. There were four or five adults in the place at the time, and they didn't know what was happening. Suddenly Hands On was overrun with kids. I ran back down to Bernie's and told him what was going on. "I need more cookies," I said.

He threw me the keys to the storage room. "Get them cookies outta here," he told me.

Over the next few days more kids kept showing up. I didn't know where they were all coming from. They must have all been talking to their friends, and now everyone wanted to come, eat cookies and run around the place. It was becoming awkward for the adults, and I began to notice that some of them were staying away. But I also knew it was hopeless trying to keep the kids away, so I talked to the adults and told them that since the kids weren't showing up until after school the adults could have the place before that. After 3:30 though, Hands On would be for the kids.

I hadn't planned on running a kid's ministry, but that's what it was becoming. I didn't feel like I knew how to treat kids, but from the way I had been raised I knew how *not* to treat them. I thought to myself, "I'll just let the little brats come in and hit the bags a few times, and I'll feed them cookies." That's as simple as my thinking was at first, but I just knew I couldn't turn them away. They were working their way into my heart. Over the next few weeks I brought in some games and toys, and I started making more juice than coffee.

Those first six kids came around every day. Lloyd was the youngest of the bunch, and a little fireball. There was also Hanna, Colin, Clinton, Jay and Jewels. From what I could tell, they were all cousins, hanging around together all the time and looking out for each other.

With all the kids coming around I needed more volunteers, but that wasn't a problem at all. Between the churches and the

Bible school I had all the help I needed. As word about Hands On got around churches from several different denominations all around the city started sending volunteers. There were always at least two or three volunteers there whenever Hands On was open.

That spring the Shriner's Circus came to the city, and I decided it might be fun to take a few of the kids from Hands On to see it. Of course, Lloyd was one of the first to claim his spot—he wasn't going to miss this for anything. As it turned out, this was the first time for all ten of the kids I took going to the circus. Lloyd was at the front of the pack when we got to our seats, and he quickly rushed along the row, taking the seat farthest from the aisle. Seated next to him was a boy and his mom, and the boy was munching away on French fries. He looked to be about 10 years old, and he was a lot bigger than Lloyd, who was only seven and fairly small for his age.

I had planned on sitting right by the aisle to keep an eye on all the kids, so I wasn't too sure it was a good idea to have Lloyd sitting that far away from me. But since a parent was sitting nearby, I thought it would be okay. I should have thought that one through a bit more carefully. Before the rest of the kids were even in their seats, a bit of an issue was already developing. Lloyd was lustily eyeing the French fries that the boy beside him had, and when the boy noticed Lloyd watching him he pretended to start feeding one to Lloyd. Lloyd licked his lips and opened his mouth—he could almost taste that French fry. Then, at the last second, the boy quickly pulled it away and stuffed it into his own mouth.

Instantly, Lloyd lost it. He jumped to his feet, grabbed the kid by his hair, pulled his head forward and started feeding him uppercuts to the face. I scrambled over the other kids as fast as I could, reached for Lloyd and pulled him away, his legs and fists still flailing wildly into the air. I had to hold him up above the crowd so he wouldn't kick anyone else. "Let me at him, Rick!" he yelled, "Let me at him!"

Just about everyone close enough to watch this scene was splitting a gut laughing at the sight of this little kid losing it on the bigger kid. It was like the circus had started 10 minutes early, in our section. The boy's mom was mad, and the ushers came over to see what all the commotion was about. Several people who had seen the whole thing unfold spoke up in Lloyd's defense, saying he had been provoked. I got my kids all settled down, and promised I would give them all a ride on the elephant at the end of the circus if they behaved themselves. Lloyd now sat beside me, and everything was fine after that. I loved that kid. In some ways he reminded me of myself 30 years earlier.

That wasn't the only incident with Lloyd. A while later I was invited to attend the annual Mayor's Prayer Breakfast as a representative of Saskatoon's street ministries. Allan Rice, an NFL running back, was the keynote speaker. Just before he spoke those of us representing various ministries were introduced, and each was given a few seconds just to acknowledge the crowd and say a few words. When they introduced me I had been instructed to say, "Hi, I'm Rick Langlais from Hands On Street Ministry...Welcome to Saskatoon." I did say that, but then before sitting down I quickly turned to Allan Rice and added, "I told the kids you were in town and would be stopping in this afternoon to say hi. Does 2:30 or 3:00 sound good to you?" I kind of put him on the spot, but I figured it was worth a shot.

That afternoon there were a lot of kids hanging around Hands On waiting to meet the big football star. Like usual, Lloyd was bouncing off the walls. I was in the back of the room when Lloyd suddenly ran towards me in a panic, screaming, "Rick, Rick, Rick!"

I knelt down and grabbed him. "What is it, buddy?" I said. "What's the matter?"

"Rick, there's niggers in the building!" he shouted. Lloyd was just repeating what he had heard his whole life. It was humorous, but it was also sad.

Embarrassed, I looked up and said, "Lloyd, that's Mr. Allan Rice."

Allan had brought a couple of his teammates with him. They had heard the whole thing, and they just about lost it laughing.

Lloyd just stood there, stunned. He couldn't get it through his head that these big black guys were the professional football players. He stared up at Allan for a few more seconds and then asked, "You're a football player?"

Allan reached forward and rubbed the top of his head, "Yes I am, little buddy," he answered. At the same time he reached behind his back and one of his teammates handed him a Nerf football. He handed the football to Lloyd, who just stood there looking up at him. I could tell that his mind was racing. "Catch this," he said, throwing the football back into Allan's face.

Again they just started laughing. It was clear that Lloyd, in his own special way, had already worked his way into their hearts. They handed out several more footballs to the kids, and then spent a couple of hours playing with them. It was a magical afternoon. They were great with the kids, and the kids just soaked up all the attention. It was so beautiful.

Along with having fun with the kids at Hands On and giving them a safe place to run around and play there were also the daily reminders of the pain so many of them lived with. Many came from broken homes where substance abuse was rampant, and the signs of verbal, physical and sexual abuse were everywhere. Some of them talked quite openly about it. Others hardly talked at all, but their body language, the dirty clothes and the bruises said it for them. Sometimes what they didn't say spoke louder than any words ever could have. Add to that the neglect and the financial embarrassment, and you could see that these precious children were stuck in a vicious cycle that, in some cases, had gone on for generations. Believe me, I knew.

It seemed to me that the kids were always hungry. I could tell that some of them hadn't eaten anything decent for a couple of days. When we fed them many would quite literally attack the food, sometimes wolfing down sandwiches or hot dogs so fast that they threw up. I saw that happen more than once, and I had to encourage them to slow down and take their time. There was lots of food, I told them, and it wasn't going anywhere. They could always come back for more. That was a concept some of them struggled to grasp.

Hands On wasn't just a learning experience for the kids; it was a learning experience for all of us—me and my volunteers included. At Hands On the kids were supposed to stand in line for their food and say please and thank you when we served them. If we didn't make them do that there was chaos, so the volunteers had to be pretty good at keeping order. If we didn't control the atmosphere the kids would.

One afternoon a nine-year-old boy named Robbie, who had started coming into Hands On regularly after school, came in. He was a small, skinny kid that I could tell was always getting picked on by others. On this particular afternoon, instead of getting in line for his food and waiting his turn, he ran straight to the counter and grabbed a hot dog. Iona, a volunteer from one of the churches, was helping out behind the counter that day, putting out the food for the kids. When Robbie grabbed for the hot dog she took a swipe at him and told him he needed to wait in line for his turn. But she wasn't quite quick enough. Robbie ducked out of the way, took a few steps back, and then looked over at me and grinned. "Thanks for the hot dog, Rick," he said, stuffing it into his mouth. In a couple of seconds he finished it off and went back for another. This time he knew Iona was watching for him, so he didn't go right to the front of the line. Instead, he waited for her to look away and then snuck in behind a big kid who was third from the front.

I stood back watching, and I could see how they both had a play on. He was pretending he wasn't coming for another hot dog, and she was pretending she didn't see him. When the big kid got to the front of the line, Robbie reached his arm around him and picked up a hot dog. Iona, who was watching out of the corner of her eye, quickly reached out and slapped his hand. Robbie, startled and embarrassed, dropped the hot dog back onto the platter. The other kids started to laugh and make fun of him, and Robbie immediately started to cry. There was no noise, but the embarrassment and humiliation made the tears flow freely.

"Hey, stop it!" I said to the kids who were laughing. Then I called over Robbie and Iona to talk to them. Robbie came right over, leaned against me, and stared down at the floor with tears streaming down his face. I could feel how badly he was hurting. The slap on the hand was nothing; he was quite used to being slapped around. He had told me he was always getting beat up at school, and whenever he stood in line for the school lunch program the bullies would take away his food, so there was no reason to stand in line anyway.

I was mad. Hands On was supposed to be a place where kids like Robbie would feel loved and safe. I managed to hold myself together and stay calm when Iona came over. I was sure she thought I was going to commend her for following the rules and keeping order.

Instead, I spoke to Robbie. I leaned down and lifted up his chin. "Robbie, would you mind telling this nice lady what you had for breakfast today?" I asked him.

"Nothing," he said.

"What did you have for lunch?"

"Nothing."

"So, do you mean to tell me that you had nothing to eat all day?"

He just stood there and didn't say anything. I lifted his chin again and said, "So, all day long, right up to this very moment, what did you have to eat?"

He looked up at me and, in the quivering voice of a broken child said, "I almost had two hot dogs, Rick."

You could have heard a pin drop. The kids who had been laughing were totally quiet. I told him I was very sorry he had gotten his hand slapped, and that it would never happen again in this place.

Then I turned to Iona. "Should we get Robbie a hot dog?" I said.

With tears in her eyes she looked at Robbie and asked, "Would you like ketchup on your hot dog?"

For years afterwards Iona came to volunteer at Hands On every Wednesday afternoon. I never heard her raise her voice again. She was one of the best and most gentle volunteers I ever had.

Robbie was typical of the kids that came in every day. My heart broke for them, and I did what I could to make them feel loved and secure. But the pain runs deep, and I knew that some of them would carry the scars for a lifetime. The physical injuries would heal, but the emotional damage ran deeper and would stay much longer. I cared for them as best as I could. I told them that God had made them special, and to remember that no matter what happened, God is always bigger than the boogeyman. I knew that was true—I was living proof. But there was so much hurt and pain that sometimes I needed to turn away to hide my tears.

Hands On was growing and was becoming what I had envisioned. But it wasn't all going to be smooth sailing. In the not-too-distant future there would be some rough patches, both for the ministry and for me personally. At times the road ahead would feel like hell on wheels.

CHAPTER 16

After Hands On had been operating for about two years, my life was unexpectedly thrown into turmoil. I went home to our apartment one day and discovered that my wife had left me. I knew she hadn't always been happy, and maybe there were signs that I should have seen, but I was totally shocked to find out she was gone. It threw me into a complete tailspin, and for the next six weeks I crashed hard. I closed the doors at Hands On and hit the booze. It felt like my life was over. There were a few times when I walked out onto my seventh floor balcony and thought about just ending it all. It would have been easy, and at times it was tempting.

She left me on November 24, one month before Christmas. I hated Christmas anyway. Before I got married I had spent 15 Christmases alone—I had been keeping track. It was always the hardest time of year for me, since it seemed like everyone else had families to go home to, but I had no one. The loneliness was awful. For most of those 15 Christmases I had checked myself into a hotel room, and drank and snorted the day away. I didn't *celebrate* Christmas; I just tried to make myself forget about it.

But now that I was married, I was starting to enjoy Christmas, and had actually been looking forward to this one. I had a new life and a wife that I loved, and it was going to be good to celebrate together with her and my new extended family. There was a different kind of joy inside my heart that I hadn't ever experienced before. But now she was gone, and so was any hint of the joy I had been feeling.

I honestly thought that my broken heart was going to kill me. I had seen people die, and now I really believed that I, too, was dying. The pain in my chest was so intense that I thought, "This must be what it feels like to die."

Once again I could feel the old familiar rage inside me starting to come to the surface. I had been learning how to keep that ugly anger in check, but now it felt like I was starting to lose control. I cried out to God, but it didn't seem like he was listening to me, or maybe I wasn't listening to him. Whatever it was, I was mad at God, too. Why would he let this happen?

To escape the pain and confusion I was feeling I started to hit the nightclubs and bars again. The violence I had worked so hard to suppress came back with a fury. I fought anyone who dared to confront me or even look at me the wrong way. Over the next couple of weeks people who knew me stayed out of my way. I was in a dangerous place. I think my friends were just hoping I wouldn't completely lose it, and kill someone. I was a ticking time bomb, filled with rage.

One Sunday afternoon after I ran out of booze I went down to the local pool hall and helped myself to a few bottles from behind the bar. The liquor stores were closed on Sundays back then, but I had to get my hands on something, so I just walked in and helped myself. Years earlier the owner of the pool hall and I had a bit of an encounter that ended with him lying unconscious on the floor, and I was prepared for the same thing to happen again, if need be. He wasn't there that afternoon, and his employee didn't want anything to do with me. I was out of control, and he was smart enough to just stand back and let me take what I wanted.

Pastor Ralph and Ma and Pa Schroeder were there for me through it all. I don't know how I would have made it through those weeks without their love and support. It was one of the ugliest times in my life. I was an emotional wreck, but they kept coming around, encouraging me and reminding me that they loved me, and God did, too. I knew that, but I just couldn't get a handle on what I had done wrong. The hardest part was not knowing why she had left me.

After six weeks, I managed to pull myself together enough to go back to Hands On. I was still angry and confused, and especially angry at God, but deep inside my heart I still had something to live for and a reason to get up in the morning. I told myself I had to pull it together. I knew that the people coming through those doors needed my help, but I began to realize that while I was helping them they were also helping me. They were giving me a reason to keep my life on track.

I knew I had to keep Hands On going. I had a great board of directors and a lot of good people standing behind me, but I was an emotional mess. My journaling from that period of my life is a record of the daily struggle I was going through, just to hold myself together. I was drinking way too much, but I was trying in whatever way I could just to get through one day at a time. I was angry at God for what he had allowed to happen.

I know it sounds ridiculous, but I even challenged God to come down and fight me. I remembered the Bible story where Jacob had fought with God all night long. He got his shot at God, so why couldn't I? I knew it was a stupid challenge, because God could have flicked me away like someone flicks a bug off his shoulder (that image kept going through my mind). But I had always fought my way out of any situation I had been in. I was learning to deal with my problems in ways that didn't involve violence, but it was still a work in progress. Right then I just didn't know what else to do.

By God's grace Hands On kept growing through that whole time, and more and more people kept coming. No matter how much anger or hurt I was feeling, my heart still went out to those people who showed up day after day, especially the children.

I was at Hands On for 12 hours a day, but I knew I needed something, a diversion, to keep me occupied for the rest of the time, too. The caring people around me could also see that I needed to keep busy. It was like the old Rick was trying to come back and take control. Sometimes I wondered if it was worth all the effort to keep living this new life.

One day a good friend suggested that maybe I should buy a house, a fixer-upper that I could work on in the evenings. I didn't have the money for that kind of an investment, so he helped me get the financing in place. Part of his motivation was also to get me out of my apartment. He told me later that he had been afraid I might jump off the balcony.

For that whole year I lived my life right on the edge. I was running a Christian ministry, but at the same time I was drinking heavily. I didn't know how else to cope with the turmoil going on inside me. I knew it wasn't right and that I couldn't go on that way, but I felt like I was stuck right where I was. I had hit a wall and I couldn't find a way through or around it.

Finally my board of directors gently confronted me about what was going on. They had been patiently encouraging me and hoping that things would turn around, but it was becoming obvious to them that I needed help. They could see I was getting angrier and more unstable all the time, and something needed to change. Nine years earlier I had gone through rehab, so I suggested to them that maybe it was time to look into that option again. They were very supportive. They told me they would do whatever they could to help me.

After some searching around we found a rehabilitation center in Montana that seemed to be a good fit. We contacted them, and after we explained the situation they said they had a bed waiting for me, and I should get there as soon as I could. Pastor Ralph and Grace offered to drive me there.

I wasn't too keen on the idea of trying to get across the border into the United States. There were some issues from the past that were still outstanding, so I wasn't overly confident that we would be let through. I decided that maybe if I just sat quietly in the back seat no one would ask too many questions, and it might work out.

A few days later Pastor Ralph and Grace picked me up at 6:00 a.m. for the all-day drive. When they got to my place I was already half-snapped—I wanted to make sure I was ready for the trip. Besides, I figured since I was going to be drying out anyway, it didn't matter if I got drunk once more.

The trip ended up being a bit more eventful than any of us had anticipated. Somewhere south of Regina we pulled into a truck stop for lunch. The only other people eating in the place were four truckers sitting together at a table. They were talking quite harshly and using the kind of language I didn't think was proper in the presence of a lady. Grace could see I was getting agitated, and told me several times to just stay calm. "It's not a big deal," she whispered, but it was a big deal to me. When the waitress came I said (loud enough so the men could plainly hear me), "If you can't put a bit in the mouth of those clowns over there I'd be glad to go over and do it myself."

There were a few quiet, tense moments, and then they looked over at us and apologized for their language. They took one look at me and got the message. If any one of them would have so much as smirked I would have gone over and permanently removed the grin from his face, along with a few of his teeth. Not another word was spoken by anyone for the rest of the meal.

When we arrived at the small rural border crossing a few hours later the guard came out of the building and started to talk to Pastor Ralph. After the standard questions about the nature of our visit to the United States, he pointed at me in the back seat. "Who's that?" he asked. I handed him my ID, and he disappeared back into the building.

A few minutes later he told Pastor Ralph to park his car off to the side. "I need you all to come inside so we can ask you a few more questions," he said. I immediately knew this wasn't going to end well. Rehab started to feel very far away.

As we walked into his office I saw an old picture of me on his computer screen, along with a bunch of information. He said there was an outstanding warrant for my arrest for some incidents that had taken place several years previous, when I was living in Oregon. He wasn't going to let us into the country, and furthermore, it was his duty to arrest me and bring me into custody. Pastor Ralph did some fast talking, quickly explaining that I was a changed man and they were trying to get me the help I needed.

It just so happened that the supervisor for the entire region was there that day. He made regular rounds to all the border crossings in the area, and we had picked the day he was there. I sensed he was trying to strut his stuff and show his junior officer how to handle what he referred to as an "undesirable situation." I don't remember everything he said, but I distinctly remember him calling me undesirable. I was already in a bad mood, and could feel myself getting more agitated with each question I was being asked. My answers were short and rude, and the whole situation was going from bad to worse in a hurry.

He was pushing my buttons, so I pushed right back. It got fairly tense, and a couple of times when I threatened him he put his hand on his gun. After a while they took my picture so they could update their files. Finally, I had taken all I could handle. I walked out, and said I would be waiting in the car. I don't know what Pastor Ralph said, but he had to do some hard negotiating just to get us released to go back into Canada.

Altogether we spent a couple of hours there before we were cleared to go.

On the drive back to Saskatoon I laid down in the back seat and felt the salt water burning on my cheeks until I fell asleep. Again I thought my life was over—there was no use trying anymore. Who was going to take me? I couldn't even get the help I so desperately needed. We had just driven seven hours for nothing. As I lay there I thought, "I really have made a disgusting mess of my life. Who would want me? Maybe I am beyond help."

My board of directors kept looking around for a rehab centre for me, and a few days later they found one that agreed to take me, in the town of Estevan, Sask. The centre was going to be permanently closing their doors next spring, but they would have an opening in a couple of months, and if I could dry out by then they would take me. I knew drying out would be pretty much impossible if I stayed in Saskatoon, so I called up my old Bible school buddy Victor who lived in Foam Lake, a few hours east of the city, and asked if I could stay with him. Without any hesitation he agreed to help me out. He really was a good friend who was there when I needed him the most. After three weeks at his place I managed to get my drinking under control, so in early December, just over a year since my wife had left me, I checked into the Estevan Health Centre.

The month I spent in Estevan was another key turning point in my life. Maybe the program they offered wasn't for everyone, but it was exactly what I needed.

My program almost ended before it got started, though. The Centre had a zero tolerance policy when it came to violence. That would have been hard enough for me under the best of circumstances, but these clearly weren't —I was about as volatile now as I had ever been in my life.

It seemed inevitable that I would find someone there who got under my skin. I tried my hardest for the first few days to just ignore him and keep to myself, but this guy was a real jerk. He swore at me and called me names until I couldn't take it anymore. I didn't completely lose it on him, but I did give him what he was asking for, hitting him just hard enough a few times to make sure he got the message. After I beat him up the directors told me they had no choice but to kick me out. I really wanted to stay, because I felt like this was my one last chance, and if this didn't work I didn't know what I was going to do.

I told them exactly what had led up to the beating, and then explained how this guy reminded me of my brother, who used to always call me names and punch me out (it wasn't exactly true, but I tried to make the story sound convincing). I asked them to please let me stay because I really needed their help. Eventually they relented, but they warned me that I needed to be on good behaviour from then on—I wouldn't be getting a second chance.

The program they offered was basically one of self-respect. It was about getting past the "pity party," and taking charge of my life. They taught me that as long as I kept whining about everything that had happened to me and kept making excuses for my behaviour I would never get anywhere. It was time for me to step up and be a man. I was certainly going to fall once in a while, disappointing myself and the people around me, but when it happened I just needed to pick myself up and start over again.

It was the kind of message I could understand. It wasn't a faith-based program, but the things they taught fit right in with my faith and with everything I had learned about God. God would bring about the change in my heart, but I needed to be willing to take responsibility for my choices and do my part, too. I walked out of there a month later with a determination I hadn't felt for a long time. I felt like I had been empowered to take control of my life.

CHAPTER 17

Hands On kept growing over the next couple of years. More people were coming all the time, making it necessary for us to think of looking for a bigger place. Across the street and up the block a bit was a building I knew would be perfect for us. It was a huge, two-storey building that had housed four different nightclubs on the ground floor and a pool hall upstairs at one time. It was owned by a motorcycle club, but they had fallen behind on their payments, and the bank finally repossessed the building. The place had been on the market and sitting empty for a couple of years already, but word on the street was that the club was going to be buying it back, so no one had come forward with an offer. They had put out the word that anyone who might want to buy it should probably reconsider their intentions.

The asking price of $1.3 million was a bit steep, but I thought that if God wanted Hands On to be there he would look after the details. The more I thought and prayed about it the more I started to really believe it was the place God had for us. So, one day I called up the realtor and offered 10 cents on the dollar.

A few days later I got a phone call from someone who wanted to know if I was the individual who was trying to buy the building. I told him I was, so he invited me to come down to a bar in Sutherland to discuss the matter. This particular bar was very popular with university students and bikers. I jumped in my car and made record time getting over there.

In one corner of the bar there was a sunken area known as the dungeon. It was about three feet lower than the rest of the bar, and was surrounded with white oak railing. I saw the gentlemen I would be dealing with playing pool down there, so I walked down and asked if I could play a game. A big chap told me he'd play me for $20 a game.

I racked up the balls and said, "Have at 'er." He broke, and nothing went down. Luckily for me, the balls were all out in the open and I had an easy run out. When the last ball dropped I threw the cue down on the table, making sure it didn't roll too far away in case I might need it. Then, loud enough to get everyone's attention, I cracked, "I'm Rick Langlais. Someone here wanted to talk to me?"

Instantly I heard the sound of a pool cue being swung at my head. I didn't see it, but I instinctively ducked to the side, and it glanced off my shoulder. I reached up and grabbed the guy who had swung the stick, and slammed his head down into the corner of the pool table. As he dropped to the floor I saw three more guys coming for me. The bouncer, who was a big guy, tried to come to my aid, but someone else stepped in and smashed him in the face. He picked himself off the floor, wished me luck, and told me he was calling the police. For the next five minutes I had one of the most exciting fights of my life. These guys were good, and we went at it hard. Five minutes is an incredible amount of time to be fighting at that level, but that's how long it took for the police to get there.

I kept going at it with the other three guys and, one by one, I took them out. There were multiple broken bones and bloodied-up faces; I received a few good shots myself, and my hands were pretty broken up. I had assumed the first guy was out cold on the floor so I had kind of forgotten about him, but partway through the fight he came to and climbed up onto the railing. Just as I was finishing off the last guy he dove down on me. He blindsided me and we crashed over top of a table. He caught me by surprise and cracked a few of my ribs, so it took me a second or so to recover. We were in a twisted pile on the floor, so I reached around him and grabbed him by the throat and squeezed off his air supply.

Everyone in the bar was crowded around the dungeon, and was watching and cheering us on, so when the police and paramedics came they had to push their way through the crowd to get to us. The four gentlemen involved in the altercation were all taken to the hospital by ambulance and the police. The police asked me a few questions, but there were enough witnesses who had seen how the fight had started, so they just scribbled down a few notes and left. The bartender poured me a double Kahlua, because mine had somehow been spilled during the brawl.

That was the only "discussion" we ever had about the building. There was an understanding respected by everyone involved. I had earned the right to make the purchase, so a few days later I signed the offer to buy the building for $130,000.

Ever since Hands On had started I had been regularly attending a 5:00 a.m. Friday morning prayer meeting at the Christian Counseling Centre in Saskatoon. I knew I could use all the prayer support I could get, so I almost never missed a meeting. The rest of the men in the prayer group were pretty committed, too. We met year-round, even in winter when it would dip to -35°C. When I told them I had signed an offer to purchase and needed some serious cash in a hurry one of them suggested I talk to the owner of a particular fast food restaurant in North Battleford. "He's a wealthy Christian businessman," he said. "Maybe he can help you out."

I wasn't sure how serious the suggestion was, because the man making the suggestion also seemed to have trouble seeing Hands On as a legitimate ministry—there seemed to be a few people like that. I didn't have very much formal training. Hands On didn't fit the mould of a typical street ministry, and I certainly didn't fit the mould for a typical street ministry leader. So, I didn't always think I got the respect I deserved (although I must admit there were times when the lack of respect was understandable—I still had so much to learn).

Still, I needed to find some money, so I decided visiting this businessman in North Battleford might be worth a shot. I called up my buddy Warren and told him to pack a few things. "Me and you are going on a road trip," I said. "I'm picking you up in 15 minutes."

All the way there I was praying that God would speak to this man's heart. An hour-and-a-half later we pulled into the restaurant parking lot, and I asked the girl inside if I could speak to the owner. He came out of his office and said, "How can I help you?"

I introduced myself and asked if I could talk to him about something important. I'm not sure what he expected, but he invited me to his office, and I decided to cut right to the chase.

"I heard you're rich, and I need money," I said.

He seemed a little surprised at how up-front I was. "Why do you need money?" he asked.

I explained about the kids and what I was doing at Hands On, and the building I was trying to purchase for the ministry.

He listened to what I had to say, and then asked me how much money I wanted. I hadn't decided for sure how much I was going to ask for, but I just opened my mouth and said, "$18,000." I had actually been thinking of a slightly lower number than that, but that's what popped into my head at that moment, and that's what I said.

He looked at me for a few seconds and then said, "I'll need to talk to God about this." Then he started praying in tongues, right there in front of me. I felt a little awkward because I had never seen this before (I didn't think the Mennonites I had been around seemed really big on the whole "signs and wonders" stuff). But I figured that since he was talking to God in his way I should talk to God in my way, so I silently prayed that God would give him a generous heart.

After a couple of minutes he stopped praying and looked across his desk at me. "God told me to give you the money," he said.

Warren and I hit the road from there for some more fundraising, heading west toward Edmonton and then down into my old stomping grounds of southern Alberta. I stopped in to talk to a few businessmen I knew, and followed up on a few other leads. When we got to Lethbridge I called up a friend and told him what I was up to. "Do you think you could pull a few of your rich friends together for me?" I asked. He did, and when I told them what I was doing they each wrote me a cheque for $2,000.

In a three-day span Warren and I raised a total $63,000 to go towards the building purchase, and with the help of a co-signer, we were able to finance the rest and buy the building.

I went right to work renovating the huge 12,000 square foot interior. Many volunteers were also there at every opportunity to help. It was exciting to see the renovation take shape over the next couple of months.

When the work was finally done, the results were amazing. On the main floor there was a big games area where the kids could run around and play. There was also a full-size industrial kitchen and a big eating area. We converted one of the rooms into a nursery where moms could drop off their little kids while they looked through the clothing area, got themselves cleaned up in the shower room or just took a break and got something to eat. We created a library, and a big sitting area, and we converted one of the bigger rooms into a chapel. I also put my office on the ground floor so I could again watch the kids, as well as keep an eye on who was coming through the doors. Upstairs there was a pool hall and gym for the adults where I set up the punching bags, heavy bags and mats again. I also built myself a suite in the upstairs corner facing the street, where I lived off and on for the next few years, in between renovating a few houses on the side.

I still got out to the pool halls whenever an opportunity came up, but now it was more just for fun—it wasn't a way of life anymore. I still had the occasional drink, but I didn't feel like it was controlling my life. Of course, I didn't call attention to this way of living because I knew there were some who wouldn't understand how I could run a Christian ministry and still enjoy the occasional drink. I also knew, though, that those same people didn't have the remotest understanding of where I had come from or what my past had been like. In my heart I knew that the progress I was continuing to make, with God's help, was nothing short of a miracle. I still had a long way to go, but if I was going to wait until I was perfect before serving God then I would never serve him. Who could? I was pleased with how I had grown, and with the direction of my life. I decided that if there were people who had a problem with an addict helping addicts, then that was their problem. It was God I was serving, and he was the one I would answer to. That was fine with me.

Within a few months of moving into the bigger building there were 150 to 200 people coming through the doors every day, and 75% of those were children. At its peak there were over 100 volunteers involved in the ministry, some coming in a few days a week and others volunteering a couple of hours a month. Along with the Bible school and churches, students from the sociology department at the University started coming to Hands On for their practicum requirements.

You'll find that 20th Street in Saskatoon is an interesting place at night. One night, while I was sleeping in the suite at Hands On, I awoke to the sound of my dog growling. I quietly shushed him, and listened. I could hear voices coming from outside my door, and then I heard pool balls clicking together. Eventually I could distinguish four different guys' voices. It was clear that, whoever they were, they hadn't come in to do any damage—they were just there to play pool.

I lay there for a few minutes thinking about what to do. I wanted to teach these guys a lesson about breaking in, but I decided to have a bit of fun while I was at it. I picked up my .357 Magnum and turned on the red dot scope. Then I quietly tiptoed over to the pool room door and listened for a few more minutes. When they were well into their game and not suspecting anything I threw open the door and yelled, "Freeze!"

They quickly raised their arms into the air, and immediately started apologizing and making excuses for being there.

"Shut up!" I yelled. "Get against the wall!"

They lined up and stood there, shaking. I could see they were all in their early teens and scared out of their minds. It was all I could do to keep from laughing, but I held it together and went on threatening them. "Do you guys realize what you've done?" I asked. "Now I'm going to have to shoot one of you." I could see their eyes getting bigger.

I put the red dot on the first guy's chest. He started wiping his chest with his hands, trying to make the dot go away. "Not me," he pleaded, "not me. Don't shoot me, my mom will get mad."

I went on to the second guy. "Not me," he said. "I didn't do it." Then he pointed to the next guy and said, "He picked the lock."

They each got a turn with the red dot on their chest, and they each pleaded for mercy and begged me to shoot one of their friends instead of them.

Finally I said, "Alright, here's what I'm going to do. I have to shoot one of you, so when I say "go" you all run for the door and I'll shoot the last one out of the place."

They started to go.

"Not yet!" I shouted.

They stopped in their tracks and again stood there shaking, and again I had to look away for a moment to compose myself. "Okay," I said, "go!"

You've never seen such a mad scramble for the door. They were pulling each other back, pushing each other down and crawling over each other to get to the door. They rolled down the stairs in a tangled ball and scrambled out the front door and onto the street. I went back to the window and watched them sprint as fast as they could all the way down the block and out of sight. I probably shouldn't have done that, but it sure was fun.

The following summer, we added something new to Hands On. Many of the kids we were getting to know had never been outside of the city, so we thought it might be fun to take them to a summer camp. Just a few hour's drive north of Saskatoon there's a popular Christian camp we were able to partner with. For the next few summers we loaded up a bus with 45 to 50 kids from the inner city and drove them up to the camp for a week. It was an awesome time of sleeping in cabins, playing in the lake, goofing around and again being able to love and value these precious children who, in most cases, had no idea what real love was.

I thought things were going well, but then in the summer of 2001 something happened that rocked not only me personally, but the very foundations of Hands On. A volunteer counselor from one of the churches was caught sexually abusing four of the boys in his cabin. Words don't come close to describing how absolutely repulsed and sick I felt when I found out what had happened. If I would have been alone with that counselor I'm not sure I could have restrained myself. I would have made sure he would never touch another child again, ever.

Over the next weeks and months differences of opinion over how to handle the situation led to several long-time supporters of Hands On choosing to withdraw their support.

I knew I had to take a very hard stand and send a clear, strong message. I felt that the kids—not just the kids who had been abused, but every child—needed to know that Hands On would never tolerate what had happened. I wanted them to know that Hands On was a safe place that protected them from this very thing. But, in my opinion, some of my supporters and advisors weren't willing to take a hard enough stand against what had gone on, and especially against the individual involved. The church where this volunteer was from insisted they would handle the situation internally and quietly. I, on the other hand, had called the police as soon as I heard about what had happened, and felt we needed to prosecute this individual to the fullest extent of the law. I wanted to make sure we were sending the strongest possible message about what Hands On stood for and, even more, what it stood *against*.

I make no apologies for the stand I took, but looking back now I can see that I did make mistakes in the way I responded to those who, in their way, were trying to guide me through the ugly mess that followed. I also realize now that Hands On had become something bigger than what I was capable of managing, and that the stress that had been building inside of me only added to the chaos. In the hurt and anger I felt, I made some very bad choices over the next several months.

There is still a lot of hurt and confusion about what happened, but the end result was that within a year of that situation the support we needed to run the ministry was no longer in place. We had no choice but to close the doors of Hands On.

CHAPTER 18

I knew I had to leave Saskatoon to get away from the disappointment of having the ministry fold, and from the bitterness it had left in my heart. I needed to figure out what my next steps were going to be. I also knew I couldn't trust myself, because that insatiable rage was starting to boil inside of me again. If I didn't get away I might end up doing something I would regret for a long time.

A few friends came along to help me and a buddy set up a pool hall in the town of Humboldt, a couple hours' drive from the city. I stayed there for about 10 months, but I wasn't happy. It was okay for the short term, but running a pool hall wasn't what I wanted to do, and it also wasn't doing anything to quiet the restlessness or the rage I was feeling. I really believed I had been making a difference in the lives of street people in Saskatoon, especially the kids. I kept thinking about them and wondered if I would ever be able to get back and reopen Hands On. I felt bad for the kids, like I had abandoned them, but I didn't know what else I could have done.

That winter the local police, fire department and ambulance attendants rented our pool hall for their annual New Year's Eve party. As the evening wore on some policemen who were drinking quite a bit were getting out of hand, so I told them to tone things down. They didn't accept my warning as well as they could have, and I wasn't in a very festive mood, so I shut down the party and kicked everyone out. They weren't exactly pleased about their party being over before midnight.

In the few months I was in Humboldt I hadn't really endeared myself to the local authorities, and this little incident didn't go very far towards smoothing things over. Things got a bit complicated between us after that, and it became clear to me I would need to be moving on—the writing was on the wall.

I started thinking back to my time working the oil rigs in Alberta. There was good money to be made, but what really appealed to me were the long hours of hard work. There was too much aggression building up inside of me, and I had to find some sort of release. Since I'd been away from the rigs for quite a few years, I decided to take some upgrading courses in Saskatoon before heading back to the oil fields. I took a course on sour gas and also got my Advanced First Aid and Transport of Dangerous Goods certificates.

As I was passing through Edmonton on my way to the rigs I decided to call up Leah, a girl I had first gotten to know a few years ago at Hands On when she came with a group of volunteers from Bethany. She seemed like a really nice girl, and I was impressed with how gentle and patient she was with the kids. She kept coming around to volunteer, and one day she caught me off-guard by walking into my office to ask me out. I turned her down flat. She was only 19 years old. "Thanks for the offer," I said, "but you're a little young for me. Come back in five years and we'll see."

As soon as she walked away I went straight over to Trent, my right hand man. "You keep that girl away from me," I told him. "Don't ever let her near my office again. She's too cute. I don't need that in my life right now."

After Hands On closed down she stayed working in Saskatoon, and even came out to see me a few times at the pool hall in Humboldt. The more I got to know her the more I realized there was something very special about her. Eventually she moved back to Alberta to live with her parents. So now, as I was heading for the rigs, I decided to call her up to ask her out.

We dated for the next few months while I was working in the oil patch, and were married in August, 2003. She is the most beautiful and amazing partner I could ever imagine. I still sometimes find it hard to believe that God has blessed me with such a beautiful, patient and loving wife.

When I got to the town of Taber in southern Alberta I stopped in at the Oilman's Bar, the most dynamic bar around, where all the rig workers went. I was there because my good friend Scott was the owner, and I figured he could give me a lead on a job.

Scott greeted me with a big smile and a hug. "How are you, Rick?" he asked.

"I'm good, Scottie," I said. "But I need a job."

"Do you want to work for me?" he said.

"No," I laughed. "I want to make some money."

He made a few phone calls, and an hour later I was hired onto a crew. I could start the next day.

We worked crazy hours—five weeks straight, followed by one week off. Our driller, Colin, was a guy I immediately respected. He was a man's man, who worked harder than anyone I had ever met before. He had an ugly temper, but then so did I, so we got along just fine. This job put me through the hardest physical work I had ever done, which was just what I needed. The long hours, fresh air and hard work soon began to take the edge off of my anger.

After a couple of months Colin left to work on another rig, and it wasn't the same without him. But then a month later he called, asking me to come work for him again. Without any hesitation I said yes.

Besides being a hard worker Colin was also a pretty passionate golfer, so quite often on our days off we'd head out to the golf course. We were both very competitive, and we had a lot of fun together.

I was again starting to enjoy life. I was happily married to my new wife, I had a good job and some good friends. I could feel the rage subsiding.

After work one day a few of us from the crew caught the day's top news story on TV about a First Nations woman who had just violently murdered someone. One of the guys spouted off, "They should just shoot her."

I got a little upset, and told him he didn't know what he was talking about. "I know that girl personally," I said. "She's been abused, raped and taken advantage of her whole life. Ever since she was a little girl she's been treated like a piece of garbage. So maybe you should keep your mouth shut about things you don't know!"

They asked me how I knew her, so I told them about Hands On and what I used to do. The next day the guy who had badmouthed her came over to apologize for what he had said. "You should go back there to work with those people," he told me.

Over the next few weeks Colin kept asking me why I was wasting my life on the rigs. "You don't belong here," he said. "I hate to lose a golfing partner, but if you can help those kids that's where you should be."

I had tried to put the disappointment and pain of what had happened with Hands On behind me. I had tried to tell myself that the street ministry was in the past and that I had moved on. But the guys on the crew were continually reminding me that I didn't belong there. They said I was made for bigger things, and in my heart I knew they were right.

As time went on I found myself thinking more and more about the kids I knew at Hands On. The rigs were losing their appeal, and deep down I knew I just wanted to get back to the ministry. I started evaluating what had gone wrong, the mistakes I had made and what I would do differently if I would ever get another chance. One of my conclusions was that I had spent way too much time fundraising. I decided that if I would ever go back I would leave that part of the ministry completely in God's hands. In Bible school I had read about George

Müller, who had done a lot of amazing work with orphaned children in England in the 1800s. He had trusted God for all his needs. He never asked anyone for money, but always had everything he needed. I decided that would be my approach, too. God knew my needs and the needs of Hands On, and if he wanted me to start up the ministry again, then he could raise up supporters.

I kept these thoughts to myself for a few more weeks before I finally told Leah how I was feeling. She just smiled, and said that she had been praying for the last six months that God would send me back to Saskatoon to reopen Hands On. That settled it.

I phoned Pastor Ralph a few days later to ask him what he thought about me coming back to reopen the ministry. He thought it was a fantastic idea, but cautioned me that it might be a struggle with some churches because of how things had ended. But he told me about a new church they were helping start up, called Faith River Christian Fellowship. He thought that this church might be a good fit for Leah and me. The pastor was a gentle man, and maybe we should give this place a try.

Leah and I prayed about it a lot, and wrestled with what to do. Finally, in the spring of 2005, we packed up and moved back to Saskatoon. We laid low for the first couple of weeks, because we weren't quite sure how to get started again or where the support for reopening the ministry would come from. I felt like I was starting over from scratch.

After we had been back for a few weeks we took a drive up and down 20th Street. It was hard on me, and I was feeling a lot of mixed emotions. We stopped and visited a few places, and I was surprised at how many people remembered me. Everyone I talked to seemed glad to see me. One Kookum gave me a big hug, and thanked me for coming back.

All the time I was gone from Saskatoon I had kept in touch with a few of my strongest supporters and advisors, and now as I visited with them I got the feeling they were just as anxious to reopen Hands On as I was. We were all a bit nervous, but also excited, because we believed it was what God wanted us to do.

Al, one of the long-term Hands On board members, had made sure the accountant had kept the books open during the couple of years I was away, so we were still registered as a charity. I was glad I didn't have to go through the whole application and registration process all over again.

Al had also kept going with the Sunday morning "bread run." When we first started Hands On, the Safeway stores in Saskatoon let us pick up their outdated bread and bakery items once a week. It was perfectly good food which helped feed a lot of hungry people. After Hands On closed Al kept picking up the food on Sunday mornings and would deliver it to other ministries around the city. It was nice to know we would be starting up again with some food donations already in place.

The old Hands On building had been taken over by another ministry, so I started to look around for other available buildings. Just a few blocks away a Chinese restaurant had closed down, and was sitting empty for a couple of years. The building's landlord hadn't been getting a lot of inquiries about it, so after a bit of negotiating we were able to sign a lease. It was quite a small place, but I knew that Hands On would be starting out small, and so it seemed like a good fit. The interior needed a lot of renovation work but again, with the help of a few good friends and supporters, we fixed it up and got ready to open. During the renovation people kept coming in to tell me they were glad I was back. It was especially good to see the kids. They were bigger, of course, and some of them had gotten into trouble or had joined gangs, but even they took the time to come around and tell me it was good to have me back.

One of the kids who came to see me was Harley. I'd known Harley since he was a baby, because in the early days of Hands On his mom was one of those who came around regularly. He was nine years old now, and when he found out that I was back he started showing up and hanging around every day.

One day while I was taking a cigarette break out back Harley came over to talk. He said, "Rick, you shouldn't smoke—it's going to kill you. I don't want to lose you again."

I had been a heavy smoker all my life, and at that time I was doing about a pack and a half a day. I said, "Harley, you're right, but I'm addicted and I can't quit. But I'll tell you what: if you pray for me every day for a month maybe God will help me quit."

"Okay," he said, "I'll do it."

"You have to pray every day," I said. "You can't miss even one day."

I figured that would be the end of it. I was quite sure that no kid, not even Harley, could pray about something every day for a whole month.

For the next few weeks I was careful not to smoke in front of Harley. He still caught me a few times, and he even drew a picture of a cigarette with a circle around it and a line through it—his version of a "No Smoking" sign. A couple of times when he knew I was smoking in the back room he went to the door and held up the sign for me. "Harley!" I'd yell at him, "get outta here! You're supposed to be praying for me, not teasing me!"

I wasn't keeping track of the days, but I guess it was a month later, while I was smoking out back, that Harley snuck through the front of the building and came out the back door beside me. He looked up at me, and I could instantly see the disappointment and anger in his eyes. "Rick!" he said. "You're still smoking!"

I asked him how he had been doing on his part of the deal.

"I prayed for you every day!" He said.

"Surely you must have missed one day," I said.

"No!" he shouted at me. "I prayed every day!"

"Okay, Harley," I said, "you need to give me one more day."

He looked up at me and pointed his finger right at my face. "Okay, Rick," he said in the most animated way he could, "you've got <u>one</u> <u>more</u> <u>day</u>! That's it!" Then he turned around and walked back inside, slamming the door behind him.

I went home that evening and told Leah what had happened. She had tried to talk me into quitting many times but hadn't gotten anywhere. I had always told her I couldn't do it.

"I know you love that kid," she said. "So what are you going to do about it? He held up his end of the bargain."

We were sitting by our backyard firepit. I stared into the flames for a few moments, and then we prayed together. "Okay, God," I said, "I need you to come through for me here." I threw my cigarette into the fire and then took the pack out of my pocket and threw it in, too. I quit right there. I knew it wouldn't be easy and that the next few weeks were going to be an emotional ride for me, for Leah, and for everyone else around me. It would be tough, but I decided to call up an old strategy, to "ride the pain" until I got through it. There was a time in my life when I would have thought I could never quit smoking. But with Harley's prayers and "encouragement" I did it.

After a few months of hard work, Hands On was ready to open the doors again. Everything was ready to go. It was all set up, and I had to literally just walk in the next morning and push the button on the coffeemaker. As I stood there looking around the place I was thinking about what I had been through, the lessons I had learned and how excited I was to be back. Suddenly I was struck with the thought that Satan was going to try once more to take me out. He wasn't pleased that I was back, and that Hands On was reopening, and he was going to do whatever he could to stop me. I wasn't scared, because I knew that since God had brought me this far he must have a plan for me. But before I left for home I took a few minutes to pray, and once again I gave everything over to my Lord.

Leah had asked me to pick up a few things on the way home, so I stopped at the store a few blocks from our house. When I parked the car I started to feel dizzy, so I decided to just sit there for a few minutes. The feeling got worse, to the point where I thought I might throw up. I was sweating profusely, and as I wiped the sweat from my brow, again I started to pray. After sitting there in my car for about 15 minutes I started to feel a little bit better, so I thought I would just drive home.

A couple of minutes later I was sitting at a red light on Warman Road in front of Canarama Shopping Centre when I felt my body going into convulsions. I remember seeing the light turn green and putting my car into gear. I felt like I was going to pass out, so I looked over to the side of the road to see if there was a place to pull over. I don't remember anything after that.

I passed out with my foot on the accelerator of my Mazda Protégé. The car took off speeding down the road, went across two lanes of oncoming traffic and smashed into a tree. When I hit the tree the airbag deployed, but the car kept going, and with the pressure out of the airbag I was bouncing around like a rag doll. I crashed into another tree, just missed a lamp post, and then slammed into a brick wall on the opposite side of the street. It took the firefighters and paramedics almost two hours to cut me out of the car. The whole time I was slipping in and out of consciousness. They took me out of the car through the back quarter panel on the passenger side.

Both my legs were badly bruised, I had a broken left ankle and a cracked breastplate. The worst damage, though, was to my face. My cheekbone had been shattered and most of my teeth were knocked loose. Over the next several days the

doctors performed a series of surgeries in which they put three steel plates in my face and gave me a new right eye socket. They also took the opportunity to partially straighten out my crooked nose. I now have 11 screws holding my face together.

My dog, Shea, had been with me in the car, and she sustained a few injuries, too. It took both of us a while to recover.

The doctors were never able to tell me exactly why I passed out. The best guess is that all the beatings I had taken as a child had caused some damage to my brain, and something must have finally short-circuited.

I spent 17 days in the hospital and another month at home recuperating. One month after leaving the hospital I opened the doors at Hands On. That day I was in a more vulnerable position than I had ever been in before. I was still recovering from the accident, and could hardly even stand up. It wasn't a position I was used to being in.

I had come back to Saskatoon and to Hands On in better shape than I had been in for years. The hard work on the rigs had kept me in shape, and I had started working out at the gym again at least three mornings a week. I knew that physically and emotionally I was stronger than ever. But the accident had now changed all that. I had always relied on my own physical abilities to deal with my problems and to get myself out of tricky situations. But I couldn't do that now. It wasn't "The Rick Show" anymore. Now it was the "God Show." How big was my God now? Could I trust Him?

I was about to find out.

That was five years ago. Today Hands On is still located in the old Chinese restaurant building. Hands On isn't the big, busy place it once was, but maybe that's a good thing. People still come in off the street every day, and we give them a warm meal, or some clothes, or we just sit and talk with them for a while. On a typical day, anywhere from 40 to 60 children come in and play ping pong, foosball or video games. They seem to always be hungry, so we go through a lot of hot dogs and hamburgers. I have several volunteers who come regularly, and also a couple of part-time staff who are there with me most days.

On December 13, 2009 a homeless man sat down by the riverbank near downtown Saskatoon and froze to death. The winters in Saskatoon can get brutally cold. The next day we decided to keep the doors at Hands On open 24-7 for people who were barely surviving the cold winter nights on the streets. I was shocked to find out just how many people were actually out there all night with nowhere to go. On some of the coldest nights we had several dozen people sleeping on the floor. We don't have cots, but we handed out pillows and blankets and told people to find whatever space they could.

One of the men who came in off the street was Adrian. He was in his late 60s and was fairly inebriated, but he was quiet and gentle, and needed a place to stay, so we found him a spot. He had a small backpack with him, and when I asked him what was in it he pulled out a pair of knitting needles and a few balls of wool. He started coming in every night after that. He would find a chair off to the side somewhere and just sit there and knit. When he found out about the kids at Hands On he started to knit blankets for them. He was never sober, but he never caused any trouble for anyone.

One evening while he was walking to Hands On he was jumped and mugged by a couple of punks. They beat him up pretty badly and took his backpack, thinking they might find something valuable inside. When they found out there was nothing but knitting in it they hit him a few more times and then let him go. He was pretty shaken up, and for the next while he stayed in Hands On around the clock. We talked a lot about his life while he was there. He was originally from Ontario and had done fairly well for himself in life. He owned his own home, and a few years earlier he had retired from a job he had held for many years. But when his wife got sick and passed away he started drinking to escape the pain. Eventually he lost everything, and ended up on the streets in Saskatoon.

I talked to him about the love and grace of God and told him that God could help him, just like he had helped me. I encouraged him to try to sober up and get his life back on track.

When the weather warmed up Adrian disappeared, and for the next seven months I had no idea what had happened to him. Then one day a man walked into Hands On. I had no idea who he was until he introduced himself.

"Hi Rick," he said. "Remember me? I'm Adrian."

I couldn't believe the change in him! He was clean, sober and smiling. He said he had gone back to Ontario and gotten himself straightened out.

"I've got something for you," he said. Then he handed me a beautifully knitted sweater with the Hands On logo on it. "You saved my life," he said. "Thanks for being here when I needed you."

It's people like Adrian that keep me going.

Literally thousands of people have come through the doors at Hands On over the years. Most have come looking for food, clothing or shelter, or just a safe place to sit for a while. We try our best to help in whatever way we can and to treat everyone with the dignity and respect that they deserve as a human being.

Because of where Hands On is located and the type of people we work with there are threats and challenges we need to deal with sometimes. Pimps, drug dealers and johns don't appreciate what Hands On stands for. I've been shot at, attacked with knives, pipes and clubs, and even stabbed with a syringe filled with HIV-infected blood. Once a truck came crashing through the wall of my office, but thankfully I wasn't at my desk at the time, because that's where it ended up.

I don't like to fight anymore, but if I have to I will. I don't fight to make a name for myself or because I feel like I need to prove anything. But I will do what I need to do to protect the children and the weak and vulnerable people who turn to Hands On for help.

I have a great board of directors who offer me advice and assistance. There are also a few dedicated men who come down on Friday mornings to study the Bible and pray with me. Leah and I belong to a wonderful church that loves and supports us and our ministry.

Another book could easily be filled just with stories of the people who we have tried to help over the years. Some of the stories are tragic and would tear your heart out, but there are also stories of amazing love and hope that would make your heart soar.

Felicity is just one example of many that I could share. The first time I saw Felicity she was about 11 or 12 years old. She came in to Hands On around 4:00 one afternoon, having just been horribly beaten up by some animal who had raped her. She was bleeding from her mouth and nose, and blood was running down her thighs. One of my volunteers immediately called her to my attention.

I went over to her and leaned over so I could look her in the eyes. "Hello sweetheart," I said, "Can I help you?"

"I'm not your sweetheart," she snapped back. Blood from her mouth splattered on me as she spat out the words.

"I'm sorry, princess," I said, "Can you tell me your name?"

"I'm not a princess either," she hissed. "My name is Felicity."

"I'm sorry, Felicity," I said. "It's nice to meet you. Is there something I can do to help you?"

"If you call the police I'll run away," she said.

I promised her I wouldn't call the police and then explained that there were some nice ladies at Hands On who would help her get cleaned up. She agreed to that, so I called over a couple of volunteers and introduced her to them. They helped her get washed up, got her dressed in some clean clothes and then gave her a bowl of soup. She tried to take a few sips of soup and, after staring silently into the bowl for a while, got up and left without saying a word. When I saw her leaving I said, "Bye Felicity, I sure hope we see you again." I knew she heard me, but she didn't respond. She just walked out the door.

I looked for her the next day, but I didn't see her. I wasn't surprised because she had taken quite a beating.

Two days later she showed up after school. I had been praying hard that she would come back. I felt like she had put me in my place the first time she was there by telling me she wasn't my sweetheart, so this time when I greeted her I was careful to make it look like I was just walking past to get a pot of coffee.

"Hi Felicity, it's good to see you again," I said casually. "If there's anything I can do for you, just ask." I kept walking, and she didn't say anything.

She came in every day that week. She would sit by herself and eat something, and then get up and leave. Every day when she came in I said, "Hi Felicity," and then asked if there was anything I could do for her. And every day she made no response. But every day I could see that the bruises were healing, and a bit more colour was coming back into her face.

It also seemed to me she was starting to hold her head a little bit higher and wasn't quite so ashamed.

She kept coming in every day the following week, and every day I was still having my one-sided conversations with her. In the middle of the week I walked by her one afternoon and said my usual line and then carried on my way. But then I heard a small, quiet voice speaking to me. It was so gentle and soft that it caught me off guard. It wasn't at all like the frightened and angry voice I had heard the first time I met her.

I stopped and turned to look at her.

"You can call me 'sweetheart' if you want to," she said. There was a pleading in her voice. She looked so vulnerable, and I could see the desperation in her eyes.

I leaned down in front of her, and looked her in the face. "You are a sweetheart," I said.

She looked at me with big, pleading eyes. "And 'Princess,' too?"

I had to turn away and compose myself before I could get the next words out. "Yup," I said, my voice cracking, "'Princess,' too."

We saw Felicity quite regularly at Hands On over the next couple of years. Sometimes we wouldn't see her for a few weeks, and then she would show up again. She was in a tough situation and was doing what she needed in order to survive. Sadly, when she was 15 years old she chose to stop her pain. Sometimes I wonder if there is more we could have done for her. Whether or not we could have done more she was a precious child, and it was a privilege to show her the love of Jesus while she was with us. She left a lasting imprint on my heart, and I hope we were able to do the same for her.

Felicity is typical of so many of the children we see at Hands On. They are beautiful and innocent children who, through no fault of their own, are often trapped in cycles of abuse, poverty or neglect. We do our best to let each of them know that they are loved and that God is bigger than the boogeyman. If and how they respond to that love isn't really our concern. We have the opportunity to love them and value them as the precious children they are, and that's what we try to do. That's what Hands On is all about.

Hands On is there to offer help and hope, and to show the love of Jesus to everyone who comes through the doors. What a privilege it is to be able to do that every day.

As I look back over my life there is a lot of pain, regret and sadness. My life, in many ways, is an ugly story. But looking back I can also see the hand of God through it all. And I can honestly say that if I had to go through everything again so that I could be in the place where I am, helping the people that I am helping today, I would do it again in a heartbeat. It was worth it. The kids at Hands On are worth it. I am doing what I want to be doing. I am doing what I was made for.

Rick and Leah, November 2010

A Message from Rick

I would like to take this opportunity to acknowledge the mighty hand of God in my life. I believe I am here today because of His love, and that love truly made the difference between life and death for me.

My desire in telling my story is not to point fingers or gain revenge on anyone. Rather, I have tried to point to God as the answer to the forgiveness, love and peace that I so desperately needed and sought.

Often we are convinced that the ugliness we see and feel inside is the real us, and we see ourselves as disgusting and unworthy of love. Instead, we should look at the true beauty that God has put within all of us. Maybe that beauty hasn't been nurtured as much in some as in others, but with God's gentle care and watering, it can be brought out. As we look to God, all of our flaws start to pale in light of the beauty of His love.

Is life perfect? No. But it sure is worth living! It's reaching out to bless others despite our circumstances, just because we know it's the right thing to do. Getting out of our comfort zone ain't ever easy, but neither is climbing a mountain. Maybe it's time to look past the mountain and see its creator – God. He sure makes the climb easier and more worthwhile.

Enjoy the journey!

Rick Langlais

How can you help?

Thank you for reading *Dysfunctional: The Rick Langlais Story*!
You can help us spread our message by doing these things:

Purchase the e-book and/or write a review at Amazon: http://amzn.to/langlais

Like our related pages on Facebook:
www.facebook.com/DysfunctionalBook
www.facebook.com/HandsOnStreetMinistries

Get news or send a donation through the Hands On website: www.HandsOnMinistries.com

You could also mention any of the above links on Twitter if you have an account: www.twitter.com.

Thank you!